Praise for CRAFT Thinking™

"*CRAFT Thinking*™ is the playbook senior leaders and boards have been missing. Philip cuts through the noise of AI and gives executives a disciplined, structured way to turn ambiguity into actionable strategy. I've watched him elevate critical conversations in the PDA network and beyond—this book captures that rigor."
— **Jason Odden, Board Chair & Strategic AI/Cloud Executive**

"*CRAFT Thinking*™ gives leaders what they rarely get in AI: clarity. I've seen Philip's framework in action through our work co-chairing the SoCal AI SIG, and it consistently helps executives cut through noise and make grounded, responsible decisions."
— **Fayeron Morrison, CPA, CFE Founder & President, Elemental AI Governance Strategist**

"Philip Topham's *CRAFT Thinking*™ delivers what leaders really need: a structured thinking framework to turn AI-driven change into actionable strategy. No hype, just clarity."
— **Jeff Baldassari, CEO**

"In high-stakes governance and leadership roles, thinking frameworks matter. *CRAFT Thinking*™ captures the intelligent, disciplined mindset Philip brings to the use of AI as a thinking partner in strategic decision making."
— **Ferey Faridian, Partner & Managing Director**

"In an era where tech leaders are bombarded by hype and vendors, Philip brings disciplined, structured thinking to the challenge. *CRAFT Thinking*™ captures that mindset and helps leaders make smarter moves."
— **Mike Miller, Technology Advisor and Super Connector**

"Developing *CRAFT Thinking*™ skills is like developing a strength to journey into the unknown; once you experience the joy of exploring the unknown, everything else falls short."
— **Errol Arkilic, Ph.D., Chief Innovation Officer, UC Irvine**

"As someone who trains faculty researchers to become startup founders, I've seen firsthand how structured thinking accelerates innovation. *CRAFT Thinking*™ provides a much-needed framework—transforming AI from a productivity tool into a strategic co-thinker that surfaces blind spots, stress-tests assumptions, and builds the kind of layered reasoning that separates successful projects from failed ones. This isn't theory; it's a practical playbook that elevates how we prepare to lead through uncertainty."

—Matt Hanson, Director, New Ventures; Staff Advisor to the Regents

"In a time when AI can accelerate noise as easily as insight, *CRAFT Thinking*™ gives leaders a disciplined way to slow down, think clearly, and make better decisions. Philip brings structure to complexity in a way that strengthens judgment and alignment when it matters most."

— Ryan K. Lahti, PhD, Founder & Strategic Advisor,
OrgLeader®, Author of *The Finesse Factor*

"*CRAFT Thinking*™ offers a clear, comprehensive, and well-rounded way to work with AI—the kind that visionary and committed business leaders actually need. Philip translates complexity into something usable, without the hype. The framework is useful for CEOs, CFOs, COOs, and other functional executives including IT, supply chain, and human resources. *CRAFT Thinking*™ removes the common misconception that AI is technology centric. AI is more about strategy, design, system transformation, and value creation by integrating technology, data, problem solving, and organizational transformation."

— Gary Cao, AI Advisor to Boards and CEOs

"Philip Topham's insightful *CRAFT Thinking*™ helps provide a useful framework and methodology to ensure good governance not only for immediate business concerns, but also addressing downstream consequences of current decisions and policymaking on a broader level, especially important given the rapidly changing reality that is AI."

— Thor L. Legvold, Psy. D., Organizational Psychologist

CRAFT Thinking™

A Playbook for Clear Thinking and Better Decisions with **AI**

Philip Topham

HIGHPOINT
EXECUTIVE PUBLISHING

This edition published by Highpoint Executive Publishing
For information, write to info@highpointpubs.com.
First Edition
ISBN: 979-8-9989720-4-1

Library of Congress Cataloging-in-Publication Data
Topham, Philip

CRAFT Thinking™
A Playbook for Clear Thinking and Better Decisions with AI

Summary: "Every week, another AI tool promises to revolutionize your business. Most leaders rush to adopt them … and end up amplifying confusion instead of results. CRAFT Thinking™ cuts through the noise with a simple, powerful framework that turns AI from a shiny distraction into a strategic advantage."
—Provided by publisher.

ISBN: 979-8-9989720-4-1 (paperback)
1. Management 2. Artificial Intelligence

Manufactured in the United States of America

Contents

Author's Note:

Why I Created CRAFT Thinking™

It was never my intention to create a model for effectively working with artificial intelligence. I just wanted better answers.

Like you, I was experimenting with ChatGPT and other artificial intelligence (AI) tools—asking questions, exploring ideas, seeing where they could help. But time after time, I found myself disappointed. The answers weren't wrong … but they weren't helpful either. Too vague. Too surface-level. Or worse, completely disconnected from what I actually needed.

That's when I realized the problem wasn't the AI tool.

It was me.

But here's what mattered even more: it wasn't *just* me.

I saw smart, curious people run into the same wall: Board members and executives of private mid-market companies who need a clear, non-hype, structured way to think about AI so they can govern and lead responsibly; as well as advisors, consultants, and educators who influence those executives and want a framework they can teach or adapt.

So I began to help others use generative AI. However, when I sought guidance for how to improve results, everywhere I looked, the advice in the marketplace was the same: *become a prompt engineer.*

Here's the truth: ***prompt engineering is mostly a myth.***

It makes AI sound technical and intimidating—as if success depends on knowing the right code words. But there's nothing "engineered" about working well with AI. It's not about mastering commands; it's about structuring your thinking. The best results come from curiosity, clarity, and context—the same skills that drive great conversations and smart decisions. The idea that you need engineering skills to talk to it is both misleading and off-putting.

So what are we supposed to do? After further thought and experimentation, I had one of those light-bulb moments.

The real problem wasn't the tool. It wasn't the person either. It's not that people can't think or communicate—it's that the tool can easily overwhelm them. Without a framework for how to think and ask, even smart people can lose their footing.

When you ask something vague of a human, they'll usually help you figure out what it is you're asking. They'll ask clarifying questions, pick up on context, or read between the lines. AI doesn't work that way. Not yet. Today's AI systems don't know what you meant—only what you typed.

Yes, AI systems are learning to remember and use context, but the real breakthrough won't come from machines getting better at guessing—it'll come from us getting better at saying what we mean.

So instead of waiting for AI to guess better, I took a different route:

Help people ask better.

As someone who has always been a deep thinker, this challenge pulled me in. I love patterns. I love systems. And I love teaching people how to think more clearly—because that's what unlocks better conversations, better decisions, and better outcomes.

CRAFT Thinking™ is the result of that journey.

It started as a personal checklist to improve my own prompting. Then I used it in workshops and consulting sessions. Then it became a framework. And eventually, a full method. Along the way, I watched it help business leaders and others looking to unlock clarity—whether they were writing an outreach email, exploring a strategy shift, or preparing for a board meeting.

At its heart, CRAFT Thinking™ is not about hacks or tricks. It's a way to use AI *with intention.* A way to slow down just long enough to get what you really need—and to make AI a co-thought partner, not just a shortcut machine.

If you take nothing else from this book, take this:

- Clear thinking beats fast typing.

- Structured questions lead to useful answers.

- The quality of your thinking shapes the quality of your future.

I wrote this book to shorten your learning curve. I hope it helps you think better, work smarter, and lead more clearly in the age of AI.

Let's get to it.

Philip

Preface

Artificial Intelligence is accelerating faster than most business leaders, advisors, consultants, and educators can process. Some sprint ahead, dazzled by possibility. Others freeze, worried about risk, ethics, or disruption. I understand both instincts. I'm a pragmatist who moves quickly with eyes wide open—excited by what's possible, candid about what can go wrong.

Here's a simple truth: **AI is a tool.** Like a hammer, it can build or harm. Outcomes depend less on the tool than on the clarity, incentives, and values of the people using it. When we confuse *tool risk* with *leadership risk*, we either rush blindly or stand still—and both are costly.

This book offers a third path:

- Move with clarity.
- Lead with structure.
- Think better, then build better.

The Tool Problem (and the Human Opportunity)

Across history, new tools expose gaps in our systems—governance, training, incentives, culture. AI is no different. It amplifies whatever we bring to it: focus or noise, rigor or shortcuts, ethics or expediency.

So let's bring it **clarity**.

CRAFT Thinking™ is a five-part method—**Context, Role, Action, Format, Target**—that turns AI ambiguity into usable decisions. It's not prompt tricks. It's a way to think *with* AI (and without it) so your outputs match your intent.

What This Book Is

This is a playbook for executive minds and practical professionals. You'll learn to:

- ◗ Frame problems clearly—not vaguely
- ◗ Pressure-test assumptions and surface blind spots
- ◗ Rehearse decisions before they matter
- ◗ Turn conversations into artifacts others can use

You do not need to be a prompt engineer. You *do* need to be an **intentional thinker**.

How to Read This Book

This book presents CRAFT Thinking™ within the following structure:

- ◗ **Level I—Clarity (Hindsight):** Build the CRAFT Thinking™ foundation. Use CRAFT to get relevant, complete, and useful answers.
- ◗ **Level II—Depth (Insight):** Add rigor. Challenge assumptions, compare options, and expose trade-offs.
- ◗ **Level III—Readiness (Foresight):** Anticipate. Run scenarios, set triggers, and practice responses.
- ◗ **Level IV—Mastery (Action):** Embed. Make AI a dependable co-thinker in your leadership and workflows.

Read straight through or jump to what you need. The method builds—each part sharpens the next.

Read Fast, Mark Hard

On your first pass through these pages:

1. Read quickly. Don't stop. Let your eye fly.

2. When something snags—agree, disagree, or "hmm"—highlight it and keep going.

3. Finish the book. Then return only to your highlights

4. For each highlight, ask:

Why did this matter to me?

Do I agree or disagree—and why?

Where does this hang on my "tree of knowledge"?

Your goal isn't to remember my name or every line. Your goal is to **upgrade your operating system.**

Invitation

Read quickly, **mark hard**, then come back to do the work. As the author, I hope to see copies that are torn, ratty, and coffee-stained— I'll know it made a difference. Use CRAFT to frame better questions, generate better options, and produce outputs others can act on. Start with thinking. Systems will follow. And when you're ready to go further, we'll talk about digital twins—AI co-thinkers that deserve a visible place beside every role on the org chart.

Introduction:

Why Smarter Isn't Faster

Prompting isn't about engineering—it's about structured thinking.

We've been sold a lie: that speed is the same as intelligence. That faster answers mean better thinking. That AI's greatest promise is acceleration.

But in practice, speed without clarity just creates waste.

The first time I used ChatGPT, I was blown away by how fast it responded. The second time, I realized how often I was rephrasing my questions, clarifying details, and trying to coax it into giving me something useful. The third time, I noticed I was spending more time editing its output than I would've spent thinking through the questions myself.

I wasn't getting smarter. I was getting faster at producing mediocre output.

And I'm not alone. Most people use AI like a vending machine: type request, get answer. But unlike vending machines, AI doesn't know what snack you need, what you're allergic to, or what you've already eaten that day. It just responds to the input you give it. If that input is vague, incomplete, or directionless, so is the answer.

That's the cost of speed without structure: we move quickly in the wrong direction.

The Illusion of Acceleration

We live in an age of frictionless input. Instant answers. Smart search. Auto-suggestions. In that environment, it's easy to mistake friction for inefficiency. But some friction is a sign that thinking is happening.

Friction can mean you're slowing down to ask better questions. To define the real problem. To imagine the use case. That kind of thinking isn't slow—it's strategic.

AI doesn't reward the fastest fingers. It rewards the clearest thinkers.

Which is why prompting isn't about wordsmithing. It's about *framing*.

The better you frame the situation—the context, the role, the task, the audience—the better the AI will perform. And that performance will feel fast, not because you typed quickly, but because you skipped the loop of revision, disappointment, and guesswork.

The Hidden Cost of Vague Prompts

Vague prompts don't just waste time. They erode trust.

- ⯈ Trust in the tool: "This thing never gives me what I want."

- ⯈ Trust in yourself: "Maybe I'm just not good at this."

- ⯈ Trust in the process: "AI is hype. It doesn't really help."

But clarity changes everything.

When you take 30 seconds to structure your request, you save 10 minutes reworking the output. When you define the outcome you want, you get answers that are usable, not just plausible.

I saw this play out with a midsize company that had just rolled out ChatGPT to its entire staff. The CEO asked me: "How do we get more out of it?" That wasn't a productivity question—it was a sign of deeper confusion. The company had handed out powerful tools without a shared way of thinking. It reminded me of the early Micro-soft Excel days: at least then, if your job involved math, you knew what to do. But ChatGPT isn't a calculator—it's a thinking partner.

And without structure, all that power goes to waste.

The problem isn't that people don't know what they want. It's that they don't think to tell the AI what they already know.

That's not stupidity. That's an invitation to rethink how we think—especially with machines.

The Real Goal Isn't Speed; It's Usefulness

Productivity isn't about how *fast* you generate ideas. It's about how *useful* they are once generated. That's what makes CRAFT Thinking™ so powerful: it slows you down *just enough* to get the good stuff faster.

You don't need to become a prompt engineer. You don't need a PhD in AI. You just need to bring a little more structure to the way you ask.

Naming the Fears

You may worry about bias, job shifts, IP leakage, security, or a geopolitical AI "arms race." Those concerns are real. Standing still, though, is not neutrality; it quietly transfers risk from *technical uncertainty* to *strategic relevance*. This book won't minimize risk; it will give you a way to face it with structure and judgment.

The Pragmatic Promise

We've navigated upheavals as large as this—or larger: industrial revolutions, world wars, pandemics, the internet. We adapt. And today we have an advantage no previous generation enjoyed: a rapidly expanding digital record of our collective knowledge and wisdom. More of what humanity has learned is online, queryable, and remixable. That makes disciplined thinking more actionable than ever.

But here's the deeper promise: *this isn't just about thinking better.* Thinking is the activity. *Outcomes are the point.* The outcome is using the best of humanity to create wisdom more quickly, better, and together—so that we make choices worthy of our society, our children, and our grandchildren.

Generative AI strips away drudgery—the clerical, the repetitive. That's its gift. What remains is the work that's uniquely human: *discernment, values, judgment, wisdom.* That's where leaders must live.

CRAFT Thinking™ helps you frame sharper questions and focus attention on what matters most—so the outcomes of your decisions *elevate*, rather than erode, our shared future.

Get ready to think with clarity, decide with confidence, and lead with foresight.

Level I

Clarity: Build the CRAFT Thinking™ Foundation

CRAFT Thinking™ Level I: Hindsight. "You are here."

Phase	Thinking Mode	Key Questions	AI's Role	CRAFT Focus
Level I – Clarity	Reflective (Hindsight)	What is happening? What do I know?	Organize, summarize, clarify	Structure & framing
Level II – Depth	Critical (Insight)	What's missing? What could go wrong?	Challenge, compare, simulate alternatives	Layered thinking
Level III – Readiness	Strategic (Foresight)	What might happen—and are we ready?	Simulate scenarios, rehearse decisions, test trade-offs	Anticipate and plan
Level IV – Mastery	Operational (Action)	How do we execute with confidence?	Co-pilot execution, automate decisions, support workflows	Consistent application

Chapter 1:

Context—Put This First

Start with relevant background and intent.

If there's one thing I've learned from working with executives, it's this: when someone says, "I want AI," what follows is rarely strategic.

A CEO says the words—and a dozen people spring into motion.

And what happens next is almost predictable: a mad scramble. Licenses get bought. Tools get deployed. A project gets assigned. People start prompting ChatGPT like it's a productivity genie.

But nobody stops to ask:

Where are we going?

It's not that the strategy is missing. It's that the context has gone missing.

Most leaders assume their teams already understand the business goals, constraints, and why the tools matter. But in practice, things get lost in translation—especially when AI is involved. Teams assume tools will help them work more efficiently. But without clear orientation, AI doesn't amplify performance. It accelerates confusion.

AI without context doesn't just waste time—it accelerates the wrong things.

Why Context Comes First

If you want a better answer, start with a better setup.

That's the secret most people miss when prompting with AI. They skip straight to the question: *Write me a cold email. Summarize this transcript. Give me product feedback ideas.* But AI isn't a mind reader. AI only knows what you tell it—and most people don't tell it enough.

They don't say who they are, what they're trying to do, what the background is, or why it matters. They expect the system to fill in the blanks. And while future AI may be able to infer more, today's models are only as useful as the structure you provide.

That structure starts with **Context.**

Context sets the stage. It's the who, what, where, and why before you ever get to the how. Without context, your prompt is just a fragment—a request floating in space.

Here's what context might include:

- Who you are (company, team, role)

- What the situation is (project, challenge, goal)

- What's already known or assumed

- What constraints exist (time, tone, audience)

- What's at stake or why it matters

It's not about overwhelming the AI with data. It's about orienting it—giving it a direction to run in.

A Real-World Miss

I once watched a marketing team try to use AI to generate onboarding instructions for a new hire. They typed:

Explain how our CRM system works for a new hire.

Fortunately AI understood that "CRM" means "customer relationship management." What came back was technically accurate—but totally useless.

The explanation was 600 words of generic content that didn't match their actual system, terminology, or workflow. Worse, it had the tone of a user manual, not something a new teammate would want to read.

The team's mistake wasn't in asking the AI to explain the CRM. It was in skipping the context:

- Who is the new hire?
- What do they already know?
- What tone fits your team culture?
- What specific parts of the system do they need to understand first?

When we added that context, the prompt improved dramatically—and so did the answer.

Five Questions to Recenter on Context

Before you prompt or pilot anything with AI, ask yourself:

1. What's the business problem—or opportunity—we're really addressing?
2. What context (market forces, timing, internal readiness) makes this urgent or valuable?
3. Who owns this domain, and do they understand the full picture?
4. How will we know if it's working—and for whom?
5. What risks emerge if we move forward without a clearer context?

These questions create a 10-minute mental briefing that can save weeks of course-correcting later.

Context Is a Reusable Asset

Once you build good context, you don't have to rewrite it every time. You can reuse it across prompts:

- A short blurb about your company

- A description of your target audience

- Your current project goal or constraints

Think of context as a modular block. You can slot it into any prompt to anchor your thinking and guide the AI. Salespeople, product managers, and operators all benefit from having go-to context templates they can reuse.

It's the difference between prompting reactively and prompting strategically.

Why We Struggle with Context in Prompts

Most people aren't used to explaining everything up front because when we talk to *humans*, we don't have to.

We say things like, "I'm going to the river this weekend," and people know what we mean. In Southern California, "the river" probably means the Colorado River or Lake Havasu. In the Midwest, it might mean the Mississippi. Humans bring shared geography, tone, timing, and body language into the conversation—so context fills itself in.

AI doesn't have that.

At least not yet.

Which means if you want useful output, you have to *supply the context explicitly*—the way you never had to with a coworker, friend, or colleague. That's the mental shift. It's not that you're bad at prompting. It's that AI isn't human. And it doesn't guess well.

Prompt Template: Context in Action

To effectively refine your message, consider the following prompt example.

Prompt:

```
Here's the context: [insert background] Now act
as [role], and [action you want] in [format] for
[target audience].
```

Example:

> Our company is exploring how to integrate AI into our customer service operations to improve response time without losing our personal touch.
>
> Now act as a strategy advisor and draft a one-page executive summary in clear, persuasive business language for the CEO and leadership team.

Note: This is a simplified example. In practice, richer context leads to better results. What kind of company is it—a privately held oil and gas distributor, or an international shipping firm? Is the customer service team supporting English-speaking clients, handling returns, or providing technical assistance? Each detail changes the tone, priorities, and examples the AI should use.

You'll see this structure come up again in future chapters. But everything starts with context. Because without it, even the smartest AI will give you a polished version of the wrong thing.

Coming Up Next: Assigning a Role

The next chapter examines the power of switching perspectives—and how assigning a **role** helps you think more deeply, not just prompt more cleverly.

Chapter 2:

Role—Step into the Right Shoes

**_Assign the right role or perspective so your AI
"collaborator" responds in kind._**

Once you've set the stage with Context, the next question is: _Whose
perspective matters most right now?_

This is where the second step of CRAFT Thinking™ comes in: **Role.**

Assigning a role helps you clarify not just what you're asking, but
who you're asking the AI to be and _whose eyes you want to look
through_.

It sounds simple, but it dramatically sharpens the quality of your
prompts.

Why Role Prompting Matters

AI systems, like ChatGPT, are inherently flexible. They can respond
like a CEO, a customer, a lawyer, a coach, or a skeptical stakeholder.
But they only do that _when you tell them to_. When you don't specify
a role, the AI defaults to a safe, generic voice. It tries to sound
helpful to everyone and ends up being insightful to no one. Giving
the model a clear role changes the conversation entirely. It narrows
the frame of reference, sharpens the priorities, and tunes the tone
and vocabulary to match the situation you're actually dealing with.
Remember when you assign a role, you:

- Narrow the frame of reference.

- Focus the tone, priorities, and language.

- Make the output more relevant to your situation.

Assigning a role doesn't just change what the AI says—it changes how it thinks. You move from surface-level assistance to context-aware reasoning, the kind that actually helps you move forward with confidence.

Real Example: The Stakeholder Swap

A founder once asked me for help with improving their investor update. They had a draft, but it felt disjointed and overly technical. So we fed it to ChatGPT and asked:

How would a CFO read this?

What would a Series A investor want clarified?

What might a skeptical board member push back on?

Each role generated different feedback—and together, those perspectives helped shape a tighter, more effective update.

The lesson? Prompting AI with a role isn't just a style tweak. It's a way to simulate stakeholder feedback before you hit send.

You Can Use Role Two Ways

The "R" in CRAFT—Role—is about perspective. It's how you shape the lens through which the AI sees the problem. Assigning a role gives structure to its reasoning and helps you explore your challenge from angles you might otherwise miss. In that sense, Role prompting isn't about pretending; it's about perspective-taking. It's a way to simulate how different people—experts, customers, critics—might think, decide, or react. There are two primary ways to effectively use the Role approach to your prompts.

1. Assign a role to the AI.
Act as a product manager.
Act as a veteran sales coach.
Act as a skeptical customer.

2. Ask the AI to analyze your work from a role's perspective.
How would a regulator interpret this?
What would a junior employee find confusing?

You're not just writing prompts. You're building thought experiments—letting AI play out how different minds might respond. Beyond these two primary uses, there are other valuable ways to think about Role—each expanding how you use AI to stretch your own thinking.

3. Use Role as a constraint.
Sometimes the role defines not just who is speaking, but how they must think. Boundaries sharpen focus. A CFO must stay within financial discipline; a journalist must verify facts; a teacher must translate complexity into clarity. Assigning those limits disciplines the AI's reasoning and keeps its answers grounded in purpose.

4. Use Role as a proxy.
A role can also act as a stand-in for perspectives you can't easily access. Ask, "As a venture investor, where would you see risk?" or "As a first-time user, what would frustrate you?" This turns AI into a safe rehearsal partner—someone you can test ideas with before real-world consequences.

5. Use Role as a mirror.
You can even use Role to see yourself more clearly. Ask, "As my future self six months from now, what would I wish I'd done differently?" or "As my own critic, what assumptions am I missing?" The AI reflects your reasoning back to you, revealing blind spots and helping you think more deliberately.

6. Use Role as a dialogue partner.
Finally, Role can frame the AI as a collaborator rather than a tool. When you say, "Act as my technical cofounder and challenge my assumptions," you're not just prompting—you're engaging in a structured dialogue that strengthens your own judgment.

Each of these uses transforms role from a simple instruction into a method for perspective-shifting, constraint-building, and self-reflection—the cognitive practices that make AI a genuine partner in thought.

Role Prompting Makes You a Better Thinker

Assigning a role isn't about pretending. It's about perspective-taking.

And perspective-taking is a core skill in leadership, strategy, negotiation, and communication. By asking the AI to shift lenses, you train yourself to see blind spots, anticipate objections, and communicate more effectively.

It's like a faster version of stakeholder interviews—without filling up your calendar.

Prompt Template: Role in Action

To effectively refine your message, consider the following prompt example.

Prompt:

> Here's the context: [insert context] Now act as [Role] and [Action] in [Format] for [Target].

Example:

> Here's the context: We're launching a time-tracking app for remote freelancers who hate micromanagement. Act as a skeptical freelance writer. Write a response to our marketing email that expresses hesitation or concern.

That role-based response can then be used to refine your message, adjust your pitch, or preempt objections.

Coming Up Next: Adding Action

The next chapter covers adding **Action**—how to clarify exactly what you want AI to *do*, and how avoiding vague asks is the key to getting high-value output.

Chapter 3:

Action—Go for Specifics

Go beyond basic commands—think critically about what you're actually asking.

If Context defines the problem, then **Action** clarifies the task. It's the bridge between understanding and doing. And in prompting, it's where everything starts to go right—or very, very sideways.

Too often, people skip this step. They fire off vague asks like:

```
Can you help me with this?

Write something about our product.

Give me ideas for improving operations.
```

These kinds of prompts are directionless. They dump the burden of definition onto the AI and then blame the AI when the output is disappointing. But generative AI isn't a mind reader. It only knows what you ask it to do. If the ask is fuzzy, the output will be too.

Why Clarity of Action Matters

A well-defined action:

- Narrows the scope of the task

- Sets expectations for what the output should accomplish

◗ Guides the model toward usefulness, not just volume

Think of it like giving instructions to a contractor. Saying "make my kitchen better" is a recipe for conflict. Saying "install under-cabinet lighting and repaint the walls a lighter color to improve brightness" is a clear task that leads to aligned results.

AI works the same way.

Avoid the "Do Everything" Trap

One of the most common mistakes in prompting is asking the AI to do too much at once.

✗ Weak Prompt

```
Tell me everything we should know about launching a
new product in Europe, including legal, marketing,
competitive, and operational considerations.
```

That's not a prompt—it's a research project.

Broad asks like this lead to:

◗ Surface-level answers

◗ Disorganized output

◗ Missed insights hidden under too much noise

✔ Strong Prompt

Instead, narrow your lens. Pick a starting point:

```
Summarize the top three regulatory hurdles a U.S.-
based startup must address when launching a digital
health product in Germany.
```

This is focused. Actionable. It tells the AI *what* to do, not just *what you're vaguely curious about.*

Weak vs. Strong Action Definitions

Compare these real-world examples:

✘ Weak Prompt

```
Give me a SWOT analysis.
```

What's missing?

- ❯ No context of the company or industry
- ❯ No clue what the user wants to *do* with it
- ❯ No indication of depth or audience

✔ Strong Prompt

```
Act as a strategy consultant. Create a brief SWOT
analysis for a mid-sized U.S. logistics firm eval-
uating expansion into Mexico. Keep it concise and
executive-friendly for a board discussion.
```

Now we're talking. This action has:

- ❯ A clear role
- ❯ A specific task
- ❯ A defined scope
- ❯ A format and audience in mind

All of that helps the AI produce something you can *use*, not just read.

Action ≠ Output

Another trap: confusing what you want AI to *do* with what you want it to *produce*.

For example:

- ❯ "Write a blog post" is a Format promt.
- ❯ "Position our product as the sustainable alternative for Gen Z buyers" is the Action promt.

When you focus only on the output format, you miss the strategic intent behind the prompt. A better practice is to pair the action with the format (which we'll explore next), but always clarify the purpose first.

Try This Instead

When defining the action, ask:

- What do I want the AI to help me *figure out, decide, summarize,* or *generate*?

- Is this a task, a plan, a reflection, or a decision support need?

- What's the *verb* I'd use if assigning this to a team member?

Your goal isn't perfection—it's precision. You're shaping the job description for your AI assistant.

Coming Up Next: Format Is Function

Once you know the action, you need to decide what form the output should take. Should it be a list, a narrative, a slide outline, a pros/cons table? The next chapter breaks down how **Format** can make the difference between interesting ideas and usable results.

Chapter 4:

Format—State How You Want Output Delivered

Structure the output for real-world usability: summaries, tables, emails, or slides.

By now, you've nailed the first three parts of a great prompt:

- You've defined the **Context**.
- You've taken on the right **Role**.
- You've clarified the **Action** you want the AI to take.

But there's one subtle piece most people miss—and it's a game-changer:

What should the output look like?

That's what the F in CRAFT stands for: **Format.**

And without it, your prompt will almost always underdeliver.

Why Format Matters

Even when people know what they want the AI to *do*, they rarely think about *how they want it delivered*. That's why a prompt like:

    Explain how our CRM works for new hires.

... often returns a dense wall of text. Technically accurate? Sure. Practically useful? Not even close.

No one—especially a new hire on their first day—is going to wade through a 600-word essay about software workflows. What that team actually needs is:

- A step-by-step **checklist**

- A bullet list of **key tasks**

- Or a **slide outline** to guide a five-minute walkthrough

Without a clear format, the AI fills in the blank with its best guess. And "best guess" often means verbosity over usability.

Format = Function

Think of Format as the delivery vehicle for your thinking. You don't want a dump truck when what you really need is a carry-on bag.

A good format turns ideas into **actionable outputs**. It turns AI from a language engine into a *clarity engine*—helping you and your team take the next step faster.

Here are some of the most useful format types you can ask for:

- Bullet points

- Slide outlines

- Tables (comparisons, summaries, mappings)

- Checklists

- Pros/cons lists

- Roleplay scripts

- Email drafts

- Decision matrices

- Roadmaps

- Scenario trees

- Executive summaries

- Prompt templates (for reuse)

These aren't just aesthetic choices. They're how you make the output fit for its intended purpose.

The Formatting Blind Spot

When people forget to specify a format, they usually fall into one of three traps:

1. Too much output:
The AI gives you more than you need—dense, hard to scan, unusable.

2. Wrong style:
You wanted a slide summary; you got an essay.

3. Rework loop:
You spend extra time reformatting, editing, or restructuring just to make the answer fit your goal.

All of these are avoidable with just one extra line in your prompt.

Weak vs. Strong Prompts

Compare these real-world examples:

✗ Weak Prompt

```
Summarize customer support issues.
```

With this prompt, the AI might return a paragraph or a long list without structure—leaving you to interpret it.

✔ Strong Prompt

```
Summarize the top recurring support issues into a
two-column table: Issue + Suggested Fix. Make it
suitable for a leadership meeting slide.
```

Now you're giving it:

- A clear format (**table**)
- A clear purpose (**decision-making**)
- A target audience (**leadership**)

You just went from vague insight to a board-ready artifact.

The Producer Mindset

Good prompting isn't just about getting information—it's about *shaping* information so it becomes useful.

So instead of asking:

```
What's the answer?
```

Ask:

```
What's the right shape?
```

Because that's where thinking meets execution and where CRAFT Thinking™ becomes a true productivity accelerator.

Coming Up Next: T is for Target

The next chapter explores the final piece of the CRAFT Thinking™ framework: **Target**. You'll learn how to align your prompts not just to an output—but to an *outcome*. Because at the end of the day, thinking isn't the goal. Progress is.

Chapter 5:

Target—Prompt for Your End User

Think about who the response is for—don't prompt for yourself; prompt for who needs to use it.

We often assume that if *we* understand what we want, the AI will too.

But AI doesn't live in your head. It doesn't know who the output is for—or how it will be used—unless you tell it.

That's why **Target** is the final (and often most overlooked) step in CRAFT Thinking™. It's not about what *you* want to say. It's about what *they* need to understand, decide, or act on.

Prompting Isn't for You; It's for Them

It's easy to think of prompting as a way to clarify your own thinking. And sometimes, that's true. But in most business contexts, you're not the final audience.

You might be:

- Writing a summary *for your team*

- Drafting an email *for your customer*

- Preparing a deck *for the board*

The *real* user isn't you. And if you don't name them, your AI output will default to the only audience it knows: *nobody*.

Clarifying the Difference: Action ≠ Target

One of the easiest mistakes in prompting is to confuse Action with Target. They're connected—but they're not the same.

Element	Question	Example
Action	What should AI do?	"Write a summary" / "Create a pitch deck"
Target	Who is it for?	"For our CFO" / "For new users" / "For investors"

- **Action** is what you want the AI to *do* (summarize, translate, draft, critique).

- **Target** is who the output is *for* (board members, busy customers, a skeptical engineer).

For example:

```
Write a product update email.
```

That's an action. But who is it for?

```
Write a product update email for current enterprise
clients.
```

Now we're getting specific—and useful.

The moment you clarify the target, your prompt becomes a strategic asset.

Same Information, Different Targets

Let's say your company has just implemented a new CRM system. You want AI to help explain it.

Here's what happens without a clear target:

✗ Generic Prompt

```
Explain our new CRM system.
```

The result? A sea of features, acronyms, and configuration details. Technically accurate. Practically useless.

Now adjust for the real user:

✔ Targeted Prompts

```
Explain our CRM system to a new sales hire with no
CRM experience.

Write a short summary for the board.

Draft an internal email to the operations team.
```

Same tool. Same CRM. Three totally different outputs—each actually useful.

Tagging the Target Is Easy

You don't need a twelve-slide persona deck to clarify your target. Just include a line like:

- ... for first-time users who are skeptical.

- ... written for time-pressed execs reviewing Q3 performance.

- ... aimed at our customer success team, who already know the legacy system.

It's a simple move. But it makes a massive difference in clarity, tone, and usefulness.

The Investor Deck That Missed Its Mark

A startup I advised once crafted a slick investor deck. The visuals were polished. The messaging was strong. They landed a meeting with a group of executives, intending to *sell* their product.

But they used the investor deck.

The meeting fell flat. No clear next steps. No interest in the product.

Except ... one exec lingered after the meeting and asked, "This looks like a great company—how can I invest?"

Perfectly aligned deck. Completely wrong audience.

The team had hit a bullseye ... just in the wrong lane.

Building a Clarity Skill

Leadership isn't just making decisions—it's communicating them. It's getting the right message to the right people in the right way. Prompting with a target in mind is one of the simplest, fastest ways to do that better.

It's not a technical skill. It's a clarity skill.

And it's the final step in CRAFT Thinking™ for a reason: it turns your ideas into impact.

Prompts without targets produce plausible-sounding answers that miss the mark. But with just one line—"Write this for X"—your prompt transforms.

You stop getting average results. You start getting exactly what your audience needs.

So as you complete the CRAFT framework, remember: Targeting isn't the last step because it's least important. It's last because it *sharpens* everything before it. With a clear target in mind, your AI output becomes clearer, faster, and far more effective.

Coming Up Next: Bringing CRAFT Together

You now have all five pieces of the CRAFT Thinking™ framework:

- ▶ **C**ontext
- ▶ **R**ole
- ▶ **A**ction
- ▶ **F**ormat
- ▶ **T**arget

In Level I, you laid the foundation. You learned to write better prompts. You received decent answers. You moved faster.

You learned how to use the CRAFT framework to bring structure and clarity to your thinking. You learned how to prompt with purpose—not just to get faster responses from AI, but to produce more thoughtful, useful outcomes. That's a good start.

But clarity alone isn't enough.

Clear thinking gets you started. **Strategic judgment keeps you from going off track.**

That's where depth comes in.

After all, exceptional leaders don't stop at the surface. They know how to **interrogate assumptions, spot blind spots, and play out the consequences.** They don't just ask what's possible—they ask *what might go wrong, who might be affected,* and *what will this mean three steps from now.*

The next parts of the book show how CRAFT Thinking™ can help you develop this **second-order thinking** with AI.

> **Level II—Depth (Insight):** You pressure-test assumptions. Spot blind spots. Add layers.

> **Level III—Readiness (Foresight):** You simulate strategy. Anticipate shifts. Design for readiness.

On these levels, you stop using AI like a search engine. You start using it like a strategic co-thinker.

- You'll go beyond the first answer and learn how to uncover nuance, explore counterpoints, and prompt for alternatives.

- You'll learn how to surface what's missing—biases, blind spots, and overlooked stakeholders.

- And you'll begin to build a habit of **thinking in layers,** not just linear steps.

This is where AI becomes more than a tool—it becomes a mirror for your thinking.

By the end of the next section, you'll not only prompt better—you'll **lead better**. Because the kind of leader who can explore complexity, sit with tension, and embrace rigor? That's the kind of leader the AI era demands.

Level II

Depth: Lead with Strategic Judgment

CRAFT Thinking™ Level II: Insight. "You are here."

Phase	Thinking Mode	Key Questions	AI's Role	CRAFT Focus
Level I – Clarity	Reflective (Hindsight)	What is happening? What do I know?	Organize, summarize, clarify	Structure & framing
Level II – Depth	**Critical (Insight)**	**What's missing? What could go wrong?**	**Challenge, compare, simulate alternatives**	**Layered thinking**
Level III – Readiness	Strategic (Foresight)	What might happen—and are we ready?	Simulate scenarios, rehearse decisions, test trade-offs	Anticipate and plan
Level IV – Mastery	Operational (Action)	How do we execute with confidence?	Co-pilot execution, automate decisions, support workflows	Consistent application

Leadership Lens: Why Depth Matters Now

AI accelerates everything, leaders have to do the opposite—they must slow down their thinking. The speed of information isn't the same as the speed of understanding. This part of the book helps you cultivate the kind of **strategic judgment** that keeps pace with change without being consumed by it.

Depth is your competitive edge. **Leadership today isn't about having all the answers; it's about asking better questions**—and knowing which answers deserve to be challenged.

Chapter 6:

From Prompt to Practice

Apply CRAFT across use cases—interactive prompting, templates, and meta-feedback.

You've seen the five steps of CRAFT Thinking™:

- **C**ontext

- **R**ole

- **A**ction

- **F**ormat

- **T**arget

But theory alone isn't enough. The real value comes when you start applying it.

That's where most frameworks break down: they explain the what but leave you guessing on the how. This chapter shows you three practical ways to integrate CRAFT into your real-world AI usage— from one-off prompts to systems thinking.

And none of them require being perfect. In fact, one of the biggest misconceptions about prompting is that you have to get it right in one go.

You don't. In fact, you shouldn't.

Refining Your Prompts with Three Practice Patterns

Good prompts are iterative. The best ones start messy and get refined.

CRAFT Thinking™ gives you the structure to refine them—across three practice patterns.

1. Interactive Prompting

Start rough. Add structure as you go.

Most day-to-day AI usage looks like this: you open a chat window, type something in, and see what comes back. This is **interactive prompting**—the back-and-forth refinement of your request through conversation.

Here's how CRAFT supports that process:

- ▸ **Start with whatever you've got.**
  Example: Summarize this article.

- ▸ **Then add one CRAFT element at a time.**
  - ◦ C: This article is for our internal strategy team.
  - ◦ R: Respond as a business analyst.
  - ◦ A: Summarize the main takeaways.
  - ◦ F: Use a bulleted list.
  - ◦ T: Make it suitable for a slide deck.

Each refinement guides the AI to respond more helpfully. It's like sharpening a question until the answer becomes obvious.

You don't need to write a perfect prompt from the start—you just need to layer clarity as you go.

2. Reusable Prompt Templates

For repeatable tasks, bake CRAFT in from the beginning.

Some tasks show up again and again: weekly updates, client summaries, SWOT analyses, blog drafts, board memos. For these, it pays to create **prompt templates** that already include all five CRAFT elements.

Example template:

> **C:** This prompt is for summarizing customer interviews conducted last week.
>
> **R:** Act as a UX researcher.
>
> **A:** Analyze the transcripts for common themes and user pain points.
>
> **F:** Present findings in a table with a theme, evidence, and a sample quote.
>
> **T:** The output is for the product team to prioritize roadmap items.

Once you've built a strong version, you can reuse and adapt it.

Templates are especially valuable when:

- Sharing prompts with teammates

- Automating workflows

- Creating libraries for SOPs or AI agents

They reduce rework, increase consistency, and preserve clarity across time.

3. Meta-Prompting

Use CRAFT to analyze and improve the prompt itself.

This is where things get interesting.

Meta-prompting is the act of prompting the AI to evaluate your prompt—and suggest how to make it better.

For example:

```
Use the CRAFT Thinking™ method to score this
prompt: Write a summary of our new product launch.
```

A well-trained assistant, such as the **Prompt Refiner with CRAFT Thinking™** (https://bit.ly/crafthinkingrefiner) can:

- Score your prompt (0-10).

- Identify which CRAFT elements are clear, vague, or missing.

- Ask clarifying questions.

- Suggest a revised version.

- Invite you to iterate again.

Meta-prompting turns AI into a **prompting coach**, helping you learn and improve simply by using the system. This practice builds prompt literacy over time. You don't just get better answers—you get better at asking.

Prompting with Levels in Mind

As you develop mastery with CRAFT, you'll begin to prompt with **depth**—not just structure.

Here's how you might expand an Action prompt through second-order layers:

- **Basic Action:** List marketing strategies for our product launch.

- **Add Implications:** For each strategy, list potential risks and trade-offs.

- **Add Perspective:** Compare them from the CFO's and CMO's point of view.

- **Add Format:** Create a table with pros, cons, and cost estimates.

- **Add Target:** Make it suitable for our board's strategy session.

This is how prompting becomes thinking.

It's no longer about getting the AI to do a task. It's about using AI to think with you, across perspectives, decisions, and outcomes.

Why Prompting with Intention Matters

Prompting is a practice. Like any discipline, it gets stronger with use.

- **Interactive prompting** helps you think aloud with AI, sharpening intent.

- **Templates** reduce drift and save time for repeatable workflows.

◗ **Meta-prompting** creates a self-improving loop.

CRAFT Thinking™ isn't a one-and-done checklist. It's a way to work—collaboratively, clearly, and iteratively—with AI as a co-thought partner.

Coming Up Next: Leading in an AI-Infused World

The next chapter zooms out to reveal where all this leads. Because the real shift isn't about prompting; it's about how you lead, plan, and decide in an AI-infused world.

Chapter 7:

Using CRAFT for Elevated Leadership

Why CRAFT is a thinking shift, not a toolkit—and how leaders take it further.

CRAFT Thinking™ gives you a structure: five deliberate steps to turn guesswork into clarity. But structure alone isn't what transforms teams, companies, or strategy.

That takes leadership.

Tools don't drive change. People do.

And in an era where AI can churn out passable content by the terabyte, your role isn't to get more out of the machine.

Your role is to get more out of your thinking.

The executives, team leads, and consultants who will thrive in this next era aren't the ones chasing novelty. They're the ones building capability. Modeling clarity. Translating ambiguity into action.

CRAFT Thinking™ is your toolset. But clarity is a discipline. And this chapter is your call to use it.

Quick Recap: The CRAFT Framework

By now, you know the five parts:

- ◆ **C = Context**—Ground the prompt in the situation that matters.

- ◆ **R = Role**—Choose the perspective or expert lens.

- ◆ **A = Action**—Define exactly what you want the AI to do.

- ◆ **F = Format**—Specify the shape of the answer.

- ◆ **T = Target**—Tailor the output to the real end-user.

Together, they give you precision without overthinking. Flexibility without vagueness. They raise the quality of your input, so the output is worth your time.

But frameworks don't lead. You do.

From Productivity to Leadership

Many teams meet AI in "get it done" mode. That's useful. But it's only half the value. CRAFT Thinking™ enables two distinct modes of work.

Mode 1: Productivity (Output Mode)

Purpose: Finish tasks faster and with fewer errors

Typical prompts: Summarize, draft, restructure, translate, convert

Output: Documents, lists, summaries, code, slides

Time horizon: Immediate

Primary user: An individual contributor

Success metric: Speed and accuracy

Mode 2: Leadership (Thinking Mode)

Purpose: Improve thinking, decisions, and alignment

Typical prompts: Surface assumptions, weigh trade-offs, compare options, pressure-test plans, reveal risks, and second-order effects

Output: Clear choices, decision principles, risks and mitigations, aligned next steps

Time horizon: Near and long term

Primary user: A leader and their team

Success metric: Better decisions and sustained capability

One-line distinction: If you use CRAFT to do more tasks faster, you're in Productivity Mode. If you use CRAFT to frame decisions, expose assumptions, and align others, you're in Leadership Mode.

The Leadership Shift in Practice

Leadership isn't a performance of certainty. It's the discipline of thinking clearly when things are uncertain. AI doesn't change that; it just exposes it faster.

What distinguishes effective leaders today isn't how much they know, but how they think—how they frame decisions, test assumptions, and guide others toward alignment. The best don't delegate that process to machines; they use AI as a thinking partner to sharpen their own judgment.

Leadership in the AI era doesn't require a technical background. It requires three disciplines:

1. A willingness to engage uncertainty
2. Clarity about what matters
3. A method to bring others along

CRAFT operationalizes all three. It gives structure to reflection, framing, and translation—so you can model, teach, and repeat them across your team.

That's where the leader's CRAFT loop comes in.

The Leader's CRAFT Loop

Here's how to use the leader's CRAFT loop in practice:

1. **Frame the decision** with context and target. What outcome matters, for whom, by when?

2. **Choose Role(s)** to expand the lens. Ask for multiple expert views if the call is complex.

3. **Specify Actions** that compare, stress-test, and synthesize options—not just produce artifacts.

4. **Set Formats** that force clarity: a decision memo, risks table, 30/90-day plan, KPI list.

5. **Align to the Target** again. Tailor to the actual audience who must act.

"After-Prompts" That Turn Output into Leadership

The quality of a leader's thinking shows up in the questions they ask after the first answer. Once you've used CRAFT to get an initial result, don't stop there. Add one or two of these "after-prompts" to elevate the conversation from information to insight.

- **Assumptions:** "List the top five assumptions behind this recommendation. Which are most fragile, and how could we test them cheaply?"

- **Trade-offs:** "Summarize the trade-offs across cost, speed, risk, and brand. What does each option optimize and sacrifice?"

- **Implications:** "Identify second- and third-order effects if this succeeds and if it fails."

- **Blind spots:** "What are we likely overlooking? Which stakeholders would disagree and why?"

- **Decision:** "Given our strategy and constraints, what decision would you recommend and what would change your mind?"

- **Next steps:** "Write the first three irreversible steps and the first three reversible steps."

The 10-Minute CRAFT Leadership Ritual

Leadership isn't about having more meetings; it's about having smarter ones.

This simple 10-minute ritual helps teams use CRAFT Thinking™ to frame, test, and commit to better decisions—without turning every discussion into a workshop.

1. **Context (one minute):** What are we deciding, by when, and for whom?

2. **Options (three minutes):** Ask AI to surface three viable paths with pros and cons tied to your strategy.

3. **Risks (two minutes):** Probe for what could go wrong and how to test assumptions quickly.

4. **Decision (two minutes):** Request a clear recommendation plus a 30/90-day checkpoint plan.

5. **Commit (two minutes):** Capture owners, first steps, and the evidence that would trigger a pivot.

Ten minutes is enough to replace circular debate with structured clarity.

It builds a repeatable habit: start with context, surface options, name the risks, decide, and commit.

Do it consistently, and every meeting becomes a leadership exercise—not a time sink.

Team Implementation

Consider the following useful strategies and tools for team implementation.

- **Onboarding:** Teach CRAFT as the default way to ask for help—from AI and from each other.

- **Templates:** Create two templates in your knowledge base:

  - *Productivity template:* Context, Role, Action, Format, Target. Include example prompts for drafting and summarizing.

  - *Leadership template:* Context, Target, Roles, Actions for comparison/risks/implications, Format as a decision memo, and a sign-off checklist.

- **Weekly review:** Run a 30-minute CRAFT Thinking™ clinic. Bring one decision and one deliverable. Improve both with after-prompts. Capture exemplars.

- **Tooling:** If you deploy a custom assistant, configure it to flag missing CRAFT elements and suggest after-prompts automatically.

Common Failure Modes

As you roll out CRAFT Thinking™ to the team, be alert for these common failure modes:

- **Tool-first thinking:** Rolling out AI features without changing how decisions are framed.
- **Output worship:** Equating more slides or longer memos with better thinking.
- **Role confusion:** Asking for a single expert lens when the decision demands multiple.
- **Audience neglect:** Delivering the right answer in the wrong format for the real decision-maker.
- **No tests:** Approving plans without explicitly naming assumptions and cheap tests.

The 60-Second Diagnostic

Ask these five questions after any AI-assisted deliverable:

1. What decision will this enable, and by when?
2. Whose perspective shaped it, and which perspectives are missing?
3. What are the top assumptions, and how will we test them?
4. What trade-offs are we choosing, and why?
5. What happens next week if we say yes—and if we say no?

If you can't answer these quickly, you're still in productivity mode.

A Short Case: Finance

Productivity Mode prompt:

```
Summarize last quarter's results and draft three
slides for the board.
```

Leadership Mode prompt:

```
Given last quarter's results and our strategy to
expand margins, compare three options to improve
cash conversion over the next 90 days. Reveal
```

```
assumptions, quantify trade-offs, propose two
low-cost tests, and draft a one-page decision memo
for the CFO.
```

Outcome: The first produces slides. The second produces a decision.

Capability Doesn't Come from Adoption Alone

You can share this book with your team. You can build CRAFT into onboarding and SOPs. You can even train a custom GPT to coach people in real time. Those are good moves—but capability only compounds when behavior changes.

Change doesn't happen because your team downloaded a PDF. It happens when someone raises the bar on how they think, how they ask, and how they lead.

This isn't a prompt problem. It's a leadership opportunity.

A Leadership Checkpoint

Every system needs checkpoints. So does leadership.

Before you scale your use of CRAFT, pause to evaluate how it's shaping your habits.

Ask yourself:

- Am I still prompting for output instead of clarity?
- Am I applying structure without reflection?
- Am I using CRAFT to think faster—or better?

Leaders who stop to recalibrate think longer-term. They don't just automate tasks. They elevate judgment.

A Brief Review

CRAFT Thinking™ began as a way to get clearer answers. By now, you've seen it's really a way to build clearer leaders.

When used well, CRAFT turns prompting into a habit of structured reflection—framing decisions, surfacing assumptions, and aligning people around purpose. That's what separates productivity from leadership: not more output, but better judgment.

With that foundation set, you're ready to move from clarity to depth.

Coming Up Next: From Reflection to Refinement

You've paused to assess your habits; now it's time to put that awareness to work.

The next chapter takes you beyond structured prompting into the real practice of thinking with AI.

You'll learn how to break the "search-and-stop" reflex, challenge the first answer, and use CRAFT to refine—not just respond.

Because leadership isn't found in faster answers; it's forged in better questions.

Chapter 8:

Beyond the First Answer

Why smart leaders never settle for the first response.

We've all been quietly trained.

Since the internet came of age—and especially since Google Search became our second brain—we've learned a pattern:

Ask a question.

Get an answer.

Click. Move on.

In those early days of search, we didn't realize we were being conditioned. Search engines gave us 10 blue links, and our job was to **scan, skim, select**. Not to think—just to find something *good enough*.

That behavior became so ingrained that now, decades later, even with AI at our fingertips, most people still default to **search-and-stop.**

The Search Reflex vs. the Thinking Shift

When I work with executives or teams adopting generative AI, I see the same thing again and again:

They type a prompt.

They get a polished-sounding answer.

And then ... they stop.

They assume the work is done—because their search-trained brain tells them it is.

But **using AI to co-think** is fundamentally different from using AI to *search*. It's not about getting *an* answer—it's about surfacing *better* questions. It's not about finding something to copy—it's about generating something to challenge, to reflect on, to refine.

This shift—from *finding* to *thinking*—is subtle but essential.

And most people haven't made it yet.

Why First Answers Are Seductive—and Dangerous

AI is optimized to sound confident. Its answers often appear well-structured, thorough, and final. But here's the truth:

- ◗ The first answer is rarely the best answer.

- ◗ The first answer reflects what's common, not what's wise.

- ◗ And if you're in a position of leadership, **defaulting to the first answer means you're outsourcing your judgment.**

What looks like insight may just be inertia.

Real Leadership Prompt: "What Haven't We Asked Yet?"

That's the inflection point. When leaders stop asking for *answers* and start asking for *perspective,* everything shifts.

Here's how CRAFT Thinking™ helps you break the search reflex and push beyond:

C—Context

Add ambiguity, uncertainty, or friction into your setup.

```
We're considering three expansion markets, but
our assumptions are based on pre-COVID data. Where
might we be wrong?
```

R—Role

Assign the AI to argue, resist, or reframe.

```
Act as a skeptical board member. What would you
challenge about this go-to-market strategy?
```

A—Action

Swap out "generate a plan" for "stress-test this approach."

```
What are three scenarios where this idea fails, and
what early signals would warn us?
```

F—Format

Use outputs that reveal trade-offs, not just summaries.

```
Give me a table comparing three options by risk,
speed, and stakeholder resistance.
```

T—Target

Tailor for real-world persuasion.

```
How would I pitch this to an operations team
worried about workload and change fatigue?
```

Prompt Templates: Invite AI into the Deeper Conversation

Prompt Goal	Sample Prompt
Break surface thinking	What's an unpopular opinion about this idea?
Stress-test assumptions	What's the hidden risk no one's talking about?
Explore trade-offs	What do we gain and lose if we go with this approach?
Compare divergent paths	What would a scrappy startup do differently than a global player here?
Simulate pushback	What's the most reasonable counter-argument I should prepare for?

Leadership Insight

If AI is the new whiteboard, **your job is not to admire the first sketch**—it's to keep drawing until the picture sharpens.

Exceptional leaders don't just collect ideas. They pressure-test them, extend them, reshape them.

CRAFT Thinking™ gives you the structure to go beyond the default answer—and toward the one that endures strategic scrutiny.

Why Going Further Matters

The first answer isn't wrong—it's just incomplete.

The risk isn't in using AI—it's in stopping too soon.

You've spent years learning to scan and click. Now it's time to **unlearn** that reflex, and lead with a new one:

Ask. Reflect. Challenge. Deepen.

The next great decision won't come from a single prompt. It will come from your willingness to stay in the conversation.

Coming Up Next: Seeing What You Miss

You've learned why strong leaders don't stop at the first answer.

Now it's time to look deeper—into the answers you never thought to question.

If Chapter 8 was about moving past easy certainty, Chapter 9 is about uncovering what hides beneath it: the blind spots, biases, and silent assumptions that quietly steer decisions off course.

Before you can lead with clarity, you have to see what you've been missing.

Spot Blind Spots and Biases

Leadership is the pursuit of what's missing.

There's a question every leader should ask more often:

"What am I not seeing?"

It's simple. Disarming. And often terrifying.

Because the truth is, what you *don't* see is far more dangerous than what you do.

Blind spots don't just live in individuals—they show up in teams, cultures, strategies, and systems. Left unchecked, they calcify into bad decisions, misalignment, or missed opportunities.

AI can help you see more—but only if you **prompt for friction, not just fluency.**

Most Teams Don't Prompt for Dissent

In many organizations, silence is mistaken for alignment.

A presentation lands. Heads nod. Deadlines move forward. No one speaks up—not because they agree, but because dissent feels risky, or invisible stakeholders haven't been considered.

When leaders use AI like a yes-man, it reinforces this pattern.

But when used well, AI can be the safest place to **simulate dissent, friction, and perspective gaps**—before the real-world consequences show up.

The CRAFT Way to Reveal What's Missing

Use the CRAFT framework to surface blind spots and biases.

C—Context

Don't just state the problem. Acknowledge uncertainty or complexity.

> We're planning to consolidate two departments. What organizational or cultural risks should we anticipate?

R—Role

Assign AI a perspective that naturally sees what you don't.

> Act as the HR Director. What's likely to be overlooked in this restructuring plan?

> Act as a skeptical investor evaluating this pitch.

A—Action

Prompt explicitly for counterpoints, exclusions, and unintended effects.

> What stakeholders are likely to be excluded or negatively impacted by this approach?

> Where might bias influence how this plan is received?

F—Format

Use structured outputs that invite critique.

> Give me a list of five potential blind spots, sorted by impact.

> Create a table that outlines each stakeholder and what risk they might perceive.

T—Target

Tailor to how different audiences experience the blind spot.

```
How would this change be perceived by a new hire?
By a tenured exec?
```

Prompt Templates: Surface the Unseen

Prompt Goal	Sample Prompt
Challenge groupthink	What perspectives haven't we included in this discussion?
Identify marginalized stakeholders	Who might be affected by this decision but not consulted?
Simulate resistance	What's the most rational reason someone might oppose this idea?
Examine internal bias	How might our team's background or history bias this approach?
Consider unanticipated consequences	What might go wrong if we're wrong about our core assumption?

You're Missing More Than You Realize

Let's zoom out.

Most leaders treat blind spots as internal: an overlooked stakeholder, a hidden assumption, a team dynamic. That's important.

But there's a bigger blind spot forming—and it's not inside your company.

It's *around* it.

We are living through the fastest acceleration in knowledge-processing in human history. Generative AI has already transformed how we work with language, software, and code. But just behind that wave is a much bigger one—models that can discover new materials, design medicines, simulate physics, and solve math problems.

Those breakthroughs won't trickle in.

They'll hit like a tsunami.

We'll have the gadgets of *Star Trek* before we even agree on what kind of future we want to live in. And here's the leadership blind spot: Most people are still looking in the rearview mirror. They're using yesterday's experience to guide decisions in a world that's changing faster than their frameworks can process.

We've been taught that change is linear, incremental, manageable.

But what's coming is nonlinear, combinatorial, and cultural.

It will reshape how value is created, how economies function, and how humans relate. And that's why we can't afford blind spots now— not just as executives, but as stewards of the future.

🔍 Why Spotting Blind Spots Matters

Blind spots don't announce themselves. Bias doesn't wait for a permission slip. In a world moving this fast, **leaders can't afford to be surprised by what they didn't ask.**

CRAFT Thinking™ gives you a systematic way to surface what's missing—so you can lead with more clarity, more perspective, and more credibility.

Don't just prompt for answers; prompt for tension.

That's how you lead with strategic depth.

Coming Up Next: Getting Ahead of the Curve

This chapter is about making sure we don't miss what's already in motion. But how about anticipating what's just around the corner … the events that will challenge your strategic success? That is the focus of the next part of the book: **Readiness.**

Level III
Readiness: Lead Ahead of the Curve

CRAFT Thinking™ Level III: Foresight. "You are here."

Phase	Thinking Mode	Key Questions	AI's Role	CRAFT Focus
Level I – Clarity	Reflective (Hindsight)	What is happening? What do I know?	Organize, summarize, clarify	Structure & framing
Level II – Depth	Critical (Insight)	What's missing? What could go wrong?	Challenge, compare, simulate alternatives	Layered thinking
Level III – Readiness	**Strategic (Foresight)**	**What might happen—and are we ready?**	**Simulate scenarios, rehearse decisions, test trade-offs**	**Anticipate and plan**
Level IV – Mastery	Operational (Action)	How do we execute with confidence?	Co-pilot execution, automate decisions, support workflows	Consistent application

Leadership Lens: Why Readiness Matters More Than Ever

Once you've learned to challenge your own thinking, the next step is to rehearse what happens when the world challenges you. You can't lead what you can't see coming. And yet, that's exactly what most leaders are being asked to do—make confident decisions in a world where the pace of change outstrips both experience and precedent.

In the past, you could rely on what worked before. You could pilot-test, benchmark, and iterate slowly. But in the age of AI, that rhythm no longer holds. **Change doesn't arrive linearly—it hits in bursts.**

Readiness isn't about prediction. It's about strategic preparation.

It means going beyond risk assessments and trend decks. It means asking:

"What might happen—and what would we do if it did?"

In this part of the book, you'll learn how to use CRAFT Thinking™ to:

- Explore plausible futures and simulate outcomes.

- Identify signals and friction points before they become breaking points.

- Build flexible playbooks that improve decision speed under pressure.

- Use AI not just to gather data, but to stress-test decisions, role-play options, and rehearse responses.

Readiness is where resilience, agility, and leadership converge.

This isn't about being first to act. It's about being first to know how to act—because you've already walked the scenario, challenged the logic, and prepared your thinking for what's next.

It's now time to look further ahead—with intention.

Focus: Use AI to simulate futures, build resilience, and lead through change.

Chapter 10:

Thinking in Layers to Anticipate What Comes Next

How exceptional leaders think across time and systems.

Most people think in straight lines. One idea leads to the next. One decision leads to an outcome.

Simple. Logical. Efficient.

But exceptional leaders?

They think in **layers**—not just sequences. They consider what happens *next … and then next again.*

They zoom out to see the interactions between systems—not just steps in a process.

They explore second- and third-order effects, asking:

> "If we do this, then what? And if that happens … what might that cause next?"

AI Makes It Easy to Think Fast

CRAFT Thinking™ helps you think *far*.

The first wave of AI adoption has made decision-making faster— but not necessarily deeper. Teams are generating options, writing strategy decks, and producing comms at breakneck speed. But if you're not pausing to simulate consequences, contradictions, or cascading risks, you're making faster decisions that fail harder.

CRAFT Thinking™ helps you slow down the logic, layer in complexity, and strengthen the scaffolding behind your choices.

Strategic Insight: First-Order vs. Second-Order Thinking

Here's the difference:

- ▶ **First-order thinking:** "This marketing campaign will increase engagement."

- ▶ **Second-order thinking:** "But if engagement spikes, will support tickets increase? Will our infrastructure hold? Will we be ready to convert leads or just overwhelm staff?"

It's the domino effect of leadership. Except with AI, you can now prompt for the whole domino run—*not just the first tile.*

Systems, Not Silos

Linear thinking also encourages siloed thinking. One department sees one slice. One leader solves one problem. But leadership requires you to hold multiple truths, tensions, and timelines at once.

Use AI to model interplay, simulate competing incentives, and project impacts across functions—not just within them.

The CRAFT Way to Think in Layers

Each part of the CRAFT framework helps expand your thinking beyond the linear path.

C—Context

Introduce cascading complexity.

```
We're planning to roll out AI-driven customer
onboarding. What second- or third-order effects
might arise across Sales, Support, and Legal?
```

R—Role

Bring in roles that reveal cross-functional implications.

> Act as a Product Manager, Legal Counsel, and CISO.
> What concerns or risks would each raise?

A—Action

Prompt for ripple effects and dependencies.

> Map out the second-order consequences of replacing
> manual workflows with automation in a team of 20.

F—Format

Use timelines, maps, flowcharts, or scenario outlines.

> Provide a cause-and-effect map showing short-,
> medium-, and long-term impacts of this hiring
> policy shift.

T—Target

Tailor to audiences that need to understand systems, not just steps.

> Create a briefing for the executive team outlining
> trade-offs between short-term efficiency and long-
> term risk.

Real-World Insight: Why 95 percent of AI Projects Fail

And the data back this up. Thinking in layers wins. A July 2025 report from MIT's Center for Constructive Communication revealed a staggering finding:

> 95 percent of AI projects fail to meet their intended objectives.

But the 5 percent that succeed deliver phenomenal ROI. This isn't about having better models or more funding. It's about thinking beyond the immediate task.

The report makes it clear: what separates the top 5 percent is the ability to understand AI as part of a living ecosystem—a complex web of people, processes, and incentives. Leaders in that top tier didn't just say "replace this machine" or "automate this report."

They asked:

- *How will this change impact upstream and downstream workflows?*

- *What new behaviors will this trigger?*

- *Who benefits—and who gets left out?*

- *What happens six months from now?*

In other words, they **thought in layers.**

They didn't just implement AI. They integrated it—strategically, contextually, and systemically.

This is the kind of leadership CRAFT Thinking™ is designed to support. Not tech for tech's sake, but foresight-driven transformation.

Prompt Templates: Explore What Happens Next

Prompt Goal	Sample Prompt
Project downstream impacts	What are three second-order consequences of implementing this policy?
Explore stakeholder chain reactions	How would HR, Legal, and Ops each respond if this plan goes forward?
Simulate ripple effects	If this feature succeeds wildly, what systems will be stressed or unprepared?
Model unintended consequences	What could go wrong six months after this rollout—even if the initial results are good?
Contrast time horizons	What's the short-term gain vs. long-term risk in this approach?

Thinking in Layers Builds Organizational Resilience

Linear thinking may be efficient, but **layered thinking is resilient.**

It's what helps leaders:

- Make decisions that hold up over time.

- See around corners, not just across calendars.

- Align strategy with systems, not just metrics.

And thanks to generative AI, you can now **simulate those layers before they collapse under real-world pressure.**

Boardroom AI Oversight Gone Wrong

When several well-known companies rushed to deploy customer-facing AI tools, they saw the same pattern play out. Chatbots that were meant to cut support costs began canceling high-value accounts. Recommendation engines pushed biased or inaccurate suggestions that damaged brand trust. Automation scripts quietly broke internal workflows.

Each failure looked different, but the cause was the same: linear decision-making. Someone saw a single efficiency gain—faster replies, lower headcount, cleaner data—and stopped there.

Linear decisions create faster failures.

Had leadership paused to think in layers, to simulate how one system's "win" might stress another, these problems could have been caught early.

This example isn't theoretical. It's an amalgam of several publicized AI missteps reported across the tech and retail sectors—a reminder that foresight isn't about predicting the future; it's about understanding the ripple effects of the present.

That's what CRAFT Thinking™ helps leaders do: slow down the rush, broaden the lens, and anticipate what comes next—before it arrives.

Developing Foresight

In a world of fast answers and instant outputs, **it's tempting to stop at the first consequence.** But leadership isn't about speed.

It's about foresight.

CRAFT Thinking™ trains you to **layer your logic, extend your sightlines, and lead with systems in mind.**

When the stakes are high, your depth matters more than your decisiveness. AI can help you see further—but only if you pause to ask: what happens next?

Thinking in layers doesn't slow you down. It steadies you for what's ahead.

Coming Up Next: Breaking Your Own Ideas First

You've learned how to think in layers—expanding decisions beyond first-order logic to anticipate ripple effects and systemic consequences. But seeing the layers isn't enough. The next test of leadership is to put those ideas under stress.

Before the market, your board, or your team exposes the weak spots, you can do it yourself—with AI as your pressure-testing partner.

In the next chapter, you'll learn how to simulate dissent, friction, and failure scenarios using CRAFT Thinking™. You'll see how to transform AI from a polite assistant into a rigorous sparring partner—one that strengthens your ideas before reality does.

Chapter 11:

Pressure-Testing with AI

How to use AI to challenge your own ideas before the market does.

There's a moment in every leadership decision where doubt creeps in.

- *Did we move too fast?*

- *What did we overlook?*

- *Will this actually hold up under pressure?*

You might trust your gut.

You might bring it to your team.

But now, you can also bring it to AI.

CRAFT Thinking™ makes it possible to simulate friction, dissent, and failure scenarios—on demand, and without the cost of real-world fallout. This chapter shows you how to use generative AI as a **pressure-testing partner**, not just a planning assistant.

From Strategy Generator to Stress-Tester

Most people prompt AI to help them plan:

```
Write a 5-step rollout strategy for our new AI
integration.
```

Few prompt it to punch holes in the idea:

> Where will this strategy likely fail under real-world pressure?

The second question? That's leadership.

Because when the stakes are high, **it's not just about building the plan—it's about breaking it before reality does.**

A Wind Tunnel for Ideas

Aerospace engineers don't build aircraft and launch them directly into the sky. They put them through simulations. Wind tunnels. Pressure chambers. They assume stress will come—and they design for it.

Leaders should do the same.

- Put your ideas in a mental wind tunnel.
- Expose them to extreme scenarios, hostile stakeholders, misaligned incentives, and worst-case timing.
- Let the structure shake before it collapses.

With CRAFT Thinking™, you can prompt AI to be the crosswind.

The CRAFT Way to Pressure-Test Your Thinking

Use the CRAFT framework to pressure-test your thinking. Here are some sample prompts for doing that effectively. (These are just a starting point.)

C—Context

Frame the decision under stress or uncertainty.

> We're preparing a customer migration to our new pricing model. What could go wrong if economic conditions worsen or competitors undercut us?

R—Role

Assign AI to act as an internal critic, adversary, or dissenter.

> Act as a risk manager reviewing this plan under regulatory scrutiny.

```
Act as a board member skeptical about our interna-
tional expansion timeline.
```

A—Action

Prompt for failure scenarios, contradictory data, or stakeholder resistance.

```
List five reasons why this change initiative might
fail or stall out.
```

```
What objections might the operations team raise
during implementation?
```

F—Format

Use structured analysis formats that surface risk.

```
Create a table comparing plan assumptions vs.
potential breakdowns.
```

```
Summarize in memo format why a skeptic would advise
against this move.
```

T—Target

Tailor the critique to a real-world decision-maker.

```
Prepare a brief that anticipates questions from the
CFO and General Counsel.
```

```
Simulate a debate between Sales and Product over
this feature delay.
```

Prompt Templates: Break It Before It Breaks You

Prompt Goal	Sample Prompt
Simulate critical feedback	Act as a skeptical advisor. What would you question about this plan?
Reveal overlooked risks	What failure modes are not being considered here?
Stress-test assumptions	Which assumption, if wrong, would undermine the entire strategy?
Model conflicting incentives	How would Legal, Marketing, and Compliance view this timeline differently?
Expose cultural friction	What team-level dynamics could cause this rollout to struggle?

Need help sharpening your questions or exploring from different angles?

See *Appendix B: Say It Smarter: —Finding the Right Language* to simulate, uncover, reframe, and stress-test your ideas.

Strategic Insight: Use AI to "Argue with Yourself"

Pressure-testing isn't about pessimism—it's about **proactive realism.** It's about learning to challenge your own thinking *before* reality does.

In today's fast-moving environment, leaders don't always have the luxury of extended deliberation. That's why prompting AI to role-play your critic, simulate friction, or model resistance is so powerful.

It gives you **controlled confrontation.**

The Board Chair and the Unasked Question

Picture this: a midsize technology company's board gathers to review a bold expansion plan into Europe. The CEO's deck is polished, the numbers look strong, and the directors nod in approval. There's a quiet satisfaction in the room—no dissent, no hesitation.

Then, before the vote, the board chair pauses.

"Let's have AI play devil's advocate," she says.

She opens ChatGPT and types:

Act as a skeptical investor. What would concern you about this expansion plan?

In less than a minute, the model highlights three overlooked risks: currency fluctuations, regional labor laws, and slow B2B payment cycles. The insights are obvious in hindsight—but they weren't in the board packet.

The conversation that followed changed everything. Instead of rubber-stamping the proposal, the board added a six-month phased rollout, new risk controls, and a contingency fund for market volatility.

Was this story real? No. Could it be? Absolutely—and increasingly, it is.

Boards and executive teams are learning that AI can play the role of the missing voice in the room. It doesn't replace judgment, but it strengthens it—especially when the social pressure to agree is high.

That single question reframed how this fictional board (and many real ones) approached strategic oversight. AI didn't make them cautious. It made them curious.

Why Pressure-Testing Matters

We're entering an era where ideas move faster than organizations can react. The cost of unchallenged thinking is only going up.

CRAFT Thinking™ gives you a structure to poke holes before others do. It helps you become the kind of leader who builds ideas strong enough to withstand real-world complexity.

Don't just plan. Pressure-test.

That's how you will forge resilient leadership.

Coming Up Next: Rehearsing the Future

Once you've pressure-tested your ideas and shored up their weak points, the next challenge is to see further ahead.

Great leaders don't just respond to what's happening—they rehearse what could happen next. Chapter 12 takes you into the practice of scenario shaping: using AI to explore multiple plausible futures, identify early warning signals, and prepare adaptive strategies before change arrives.

It's where CRAFT Thinking™ becomes a foresight tool—helping you and your organization move from reactive planning to proactive readiness.

Chapter 12:

Shape Scenarios with AI

Use strategic foresight to prepare before reality arrives.

When uncertainty rises, leaders default to one of two instincts:

1. Wait and see.

2. Do what worked last time.

Both are dangerous in an era where the future isn't just unfamiliar—it's fundamentally *different*. This is where scenario thinking comes in.

It's not about predicting the future. It's about preparing for multiple plausible futures.

CRAFT Thinking™ helps leaders use AI to explore, contrast, and rehearse potential futures—so when change happens, it feels more like déjà vu than surprise.

Scenario Thinking: A New Core Skill for Leadership

Strategy used to be about picking a direction and committing to it. Today, it's about holding multiple directional possibilities in your mind—and knowing what action you'd take under each.

That's not ambiguity. That's **agility.**

The best leaders don't make decisions at the last possible second.

They make pre-decisions—with contingency logic, trigger points, and flexible playbooks.

With AI, you can build these thought experiments in minutes.

Scenario Thinking

Concept	What It Is	Its Limitations	CRAFT Leadership Upgrade
Forecasting	Predicting what's likely to happen based on past trends or current data	Assumes continuity; breaks under volatility	Use AI to identify signals, but don't rely solely on one path
Scenario Planning	Exploring multiple plausible futures—what could happen	Often abstract or one-time exercises	Use CRAFT to simulate impacts and tailor responses
Strategic Readiness	Being mentally and organizationally prepared to act under any scenario	Requires systems, training, and decision frameworks	CRAFT helps you rehearse decision-making before it's needed

Why AI Supercharges Scenario Thinking

In the past, scenario planning was a slow, expensive process. It involved consultants, war rooms, and workshops. Now, it's accessible to anyone who can structure a thought and prompt clearly.

With the right framing, AI can help you:

▶ Generate multiple plausible futures based on current trends.

▶ Simulate how decisions play out across markets, stakeholders, or time horizons.

▶ Explore unexpected consequences before they show up in reality.

▶ Practice how you (or your team) might respond under pressure.

The key isn't automation—it's imagination, structured by CRAFT.

The CRAFT Way to Shape Scenarios

Use the CRAFT framework to shape scenarios.

C—Context

Set up an open-ended situation, not a decision request.

> We're entering a new market with uncertain regulatory conditions. What are three plausible future scenarios—best case, worst case, and wildcard?

R—Role

Ask AI to adopt future-facing or strategic roles.

> Act as a geopolitical analyst advising a CEO in 2027. What are the likely consequences of AI regulation on cross-border operations?

A—Action

Ask for scenario construction, divergence modeling, or ripple effects.

> Develop three scenarios for how generative AI (GenAI) adoption could impact our pricing model by 2028.

F—Format

Use timelines, if/then trees, or scenario matrices.

> Provide a 3 x 3 matrix of scenarios based on internal alignment (low/high) and market volatility (low/medium/high).

T—Target

Tailor the scenario output for leadership decisions.

> Present these scenarios in a board briefing format with strategic implications and early warning signals.

Prompt Templates: Explore the What-Ifs

Prompt Goal	Sample Prompt
Generate future narratives	What are three ways AI could change our hiring practices by 2030?
Model cascading change	If supply chain friction continues, how might our margins, staffing, and pricing shift over two years?
Explore trigger-based decisions	If customer growth hits 25% in Q1, what should we be doing differently by Q2?
Design contingency paths	What are two possible product roadmaps depending on interest rate trends?
Combine signals into scenarios	Based on current trends in labor, regulation, and tech, outline three strategic future states for our industry.

Strategic Insight: Don't Just Monitor—Mentally Rehearse

Most companies monitor indicators. Few rehearse what they'll actually do if those indicators shift.

Scenario thinking isn't about predicting the future—it's about **rehearsing your leadership in advance.** When you pair that with AI, you can run low-cost, high-value mental simulations that help you make faster, clearer decisions when it counts.

> If you've *already thought the future through*, you'll act with more calm, confidence, and clarity.

Why Scenario-Shaping Matters

Foresight isn't a luxury. It's a leadership competency. And it's no longer reserved for long-range planners or innovation labs.

With the right mindset and structure, you can use CRAFT Thinking™ to make scenario exploration a habit—not a panic response.

Don't wait for the future to arrive. *Think through it now—so when it shows up, you're ready.*

Coming Up Next: From Readiness to Real-Time Judgment

Readiness is the bridge between preparation and performance—but leadership mastery means knowing when to act, not just how. The next chapter explores how to translate your pre-modeled options into confident real-time judgment. You'll learn how CRAFT Thinking™ helps leaders stay centered when circumstances shift mid-decision—using AI not to predict, but to clarify, recalibrate, and choose with precision under pressure.

Level IV

Mastery: Embed AI Into How You Lead

CRAFT Thinking™ Level IV: Action. "You are here."

Phase	Thinking Mode	Key Questions	AI's Role	CRAFT Focus
Level I – Clarity	Reflective (Hindsight)	What is happening? What do I know?	Organize, summarize, clarify	Structure & framing
Level II – Depth	Critical (Insight)	What's missing? What could go wrong?	Challenge, compare, simulate alternatives	Layered thinking
Level III – Readiness	Strategic (Foresight)	What might happen—and are we ready?	Simulate scenarios, rehearse decisions, test trade-offs	Anticipate and plan
Level IV – Mastery	**Operational (Action)**	**How do we execute with confidence?**	**Co-pilot execution, automate decisions, support workflows**	**Consistent application**

Chapter 13:

From Response to Readiness

Build leadership reflexes before they're tested.

Firefighters don't wait until the blaze starts to figure out what to do.

They rehearse. They simulate. They prepare for the fire *before* it breaks out—because when it does, the time for planning is over.

Most businesses aren't built like fire departments. And that's not a flaw—it's a reflection of rational design.

For decades, leaders have optimized for **efficiency, stability, and prevention.**

The assumption was: fires are rare. Disruption is manageable. Change moves slowly enough that you can adapt when needed. That mindset made sense—when the world was slower. But we've entered a different operating environment.

Disruption is no longer episodic—it's ambient. Fires now start outside your walls, move faster than your normal response cycle, and demand decisions before full certainty is possible.

You can't control when the next fire comes.

But you can control how ready you are to act when it does.

Readiness Is a Leadership Discipline

Readiness means you don't just wait for the signal to decide—you've already thought through what you'll do when certain signals appear.

This is where CRAFT Thinking™ becomes a powerful tool for scenario rehearsal, decision simulation, and early-option modeling. It gives you:

- A way to structure critical thinking before things go sideways.
- A shared language for pressure-testing options across teams.
- A habit of mental rehearsal, so your decisions feel less rushed, even when timelines compress.

Reactive = Slow

Ready = fast *and* informed.

When crises or inflection points arrive, they don't give you time to think from scratch. You need *decision agility*—the ability to assess, align, and act without collapsing under pressure.

With AI, you can now simulate decisions ahead of time:

- Explore if-then conditions.
- Pre-debate contentious paths.
- Draft stakeholder messages in advance.
- Build option trees with AI as a thought partner—not after something breaks, but before.

The CRAFT Way to Build Readiness

Readiness isn't theory—it's practice. You build it through repetition, rehearsal, and reflection before the pressure hits. The prompts below translate that mindset into action, giving you a way to test your decision reflexes and strengthen them over time.

C—Context

Frame the condition, trigger, or uncertainty that might force a decision.

```
If Q3 revenue dips below 15% YoY, what options
should we have pre-modeled?
```

R—Role

Use AI to simulate friction across functional perspectives.

> Act as a CFO, Head of People, and Chief Risk
> Officer—how would each respond to a hiring freeze?

A—Action

Ask for recommended options, risk/benefit trade-offs, or early warning signals.

> List 3 strategic options if our supply chain
> breaks again in the next 60 days—include risk and
> resource impact.

F—Format

Use decision matrices, playbooks, or stepwise flow diagrams.

> Summarize 3 readiness options in a table showing
> trigger, action, and key risks.

T—Target

Tailor the simulation to the people who must *decide*, not just understand.

> Draft a decision brief for the exec team outlining
> which option to pre-authorize under emergency
> conditions.

Strategic Insight: Slow Thinking in Advance Enables Fast Acting Under Pressure

Fast action in a crisis isn't about improvisation—it's about pre-considered judgment.

The best leaders aren't the ones who think the fastest in the moment—they're the ones who've already done the thinking.

CRAFT Thinking™ gives you a practical way to simulate, discuss, and align *before* you need to act—using AI to walk through the hard choices ahead of time.

Prompt Templates: Prepare to Decide Before You Must

Prompt Goal	Sample Prompt
Identify pre-decision triggers	What events would force a strategic change in our 2025 roadmap?
Model readiness playbooks	List 3 playbooks we should have ready for rapid customer growth or churn.
Simulate leadership alignment	What messaging should be ready for internal teams if we shift priorities suddenly?
Pre-model critical decisions	How should we frame a go/no-go decision if funding isn't renewed by Q2?
Explore shared assumptions	What assumptions do our decision paths rely on— and what if they no longer hold?

If you've pre-framed the trade-offs, you don't need perfect information to move forward. You need readiness.

Why Preparedness Matters

In an age of increasing volatility, leaders who wait to respond will always be one step behind. The new edge isn't speed—it's *preparedness*.

When you combine structured foresight with real-time simulation, you get an organization that can act wisely, not just quickly.

Don't just gather facts in a crisis. Use CRAFT to build the mental scaffolding while there's still time to think.

Coming Up Next: From Judgment to Mastery in Motion

Once you've built readiness and judgment, the final step is embedding CRAFT Thinking™ into daily operations. The next chapter shows how to make AI-assisted leadership second nature so structured thinking becomes an organizational reflex. You'll see how to turn one-off exercises into enduring habits, where clarity, challenge, and curiosity guide every meeting, message, and move.

Chapter 14:

Foresight Is a Leadership Muscle

Strengthen your ability to lead before reality arrives.

Some leaders seem calm in a storm. They don't flinch, delay, or panic. They act with clarity—even when the path forward isn't clear.

That's not intuition. It's not luck.

It's foresight in action—the practiced ability to make confident decisions in unfamiliar situations because you've already trained your mind to think ahead.

And like any skill, foresight can be strengthened.

You Don't Need a Crystal Ball; You Need Reps

We often associate foresight with long-range futurists or strategy teams running complex models.

But in reality, foresight lives in everyday leadership:

- Noticing early signals
- Exploring what-ifs
- Testing your mental flexibility
- Making small pre-committed decisions before urgency hits

Like muscle memory, foresight grows through repetition—especially when you use AI to simulate scenarios, explore trade-offs, and practice acting under uncertainty.

From Uncertainty to Optionality

Foresight isn't about knowing what will happen. It's about building *optional paths*, so when change comes, you're already positioned to move.

Instead of hoping for one outcome, you plan for three.

Instead of waiting for certainty, you define trigger points.

Instead of getting stuck in over-analysis, you build mental infrastructure that speeds up real-world action.

And with AI, this kind of anticipatory thinking is now cheap, fast, and scalable.

Practicing the Future Before It Happens in 90 minutes

Think of this as a thought exercise—a short glimpse of what a foresight-driven meeting could look like with AI in the mix.

When a global logistics company saw early signs of volatility in its shipping costs, the CEO called an impromptu foresight session. Normally, this kind of analysis would require weeks of preparation and consultant time. Instead, the executive team decided to experiment with AI.

Each leader took a different lens: the CFO asked AI to model financial exposure if costs spiked 20 percent. The COO explored operational bottlenecks under supply chain stress. The CCO examined how competitors might reposition their pricing. Within 90 minutes, they had five simulated futures on the table—each plausible, each with distinct trade-offs.

What surprised them wasn't the scenarios themselves—it was how quickly patterns emerged. Every simulation pointed to the same vulnerability: reliance on a single carrier alliance. By the end of the meeting, the team had outlined preemptive diversification moves that later became core to their resilience plan.

They hadn't predicted what would happen next. They had practiced leading into it.

The CRAFT Way to Build the Foresight Habit

Here are sample CRAFT Thinking™ prompts designed to increase your foresight.

C—Context

Build prompts that surface emerging tension or uncertainty.

> We're seeing early signs of customer churn. What market or behavioral shifts could this indicate?

R—Role

Assign future-facing roles—strategic advisor, market futurist, chief of staff in 2028.

> Act as a corporate strategist in 2026. What new capabilities should we be developing now to stay relevant?

A—Action

Ask AI to run the reps: explore, simulate, stretch your thinking.

> Develop three possible outcomes if regulatory policy shifts in our sector. What early actions could we take now?

F—Format

Use foresight-friendly structures: scenario maps, timelines, option trees, pre-mortems.

> Provide a pre-mortem for our 2025 strategy. What could cause it to fail, and what can we do today to reduce that risk?

T—Target

Translate foresight outputs for decision-makers, planners, and risk-owners.

> Draft a foresight briefing for the executive team with short-term and long-term implications of industry AI adoption.

Prompt Templates: Build Foresight into Your Week

Prompt Goal	Sample Prompt
Sense early signals	What weak signals might suggest our cost model is becoming outdated?
Generate next-step options	What three future-facing options do we have if our top partner exits the market?
Rehearse pivots	If demand shifts suddenly, what would our 90-day response plan look like?
Map out learning gaps	What skills or capabilities are we not developing but might need in 18 months?
Expand from a single-point strategy	What does our plan look like if the market grows faster than expected? Slower?

Strategic Insight: Foresight Isn't Prediction— It's Practice

You won't be right about every future scenario. But you don't have to be.

Foresight isn't about guessing correctly.

It's about training your brain, your team, and your systems to respond with less hesitation and more intention.

You don't develop foresight by waiting for the world to prove you wrong. You develop it by practicing how you'll lead in futures that haven't happened *yet*.

The more futures you rehearse, the fewer surprises feel truly new.

Why "Mastery" Anchors This Framework

In this model, *mastery* doesn't mean perfection. It means having the mental readiness, strategic muscle memory, and system-level habits to lead decisively—even amid volatility.

Mastery emerges when:

- **Foresight** reveals what's coming.
- **Preparation** turns insight into readiness.
- **Agility** enables real-time, intelligent response.

This cycle builds *more than knowledge*. It builds the confidence and competence to lead from the future—not just react to it.

Why Foresight Matters

The next disruption will come. It may be global or hyper-local. It may be technical, regulatory, behavioral, or all at once.

You won't be able to predict it.

But you *can* be ready to lead through it.

CRAFT Thinking™ turns foresight from an abstract discipline into a daily leadership advantage—one decision simulation at a time.

Don't just lead in the present. Lead from the future.

Coming Up Next: From Foresight to Shared Clarity

Foresight sharpens your personal leadership reflexes—but mastery requires more than individual awareness. The next chapter explores how to scale that same clarity across teams and systems. You'll see how CRAFT Thinking™ evolves from a personal discipline into a repeatable, organization-wide framework—one that embeds structured reflection, decision rigor, and learning loops into every workflow.

Chapter 15:

Scaling Clarity: From Conversations to Systems

CRAFT Thinking™ is a human-centered practice.

The CRAFT Thinking™ framework was never designed for prompt engineers. It's a **thinking scaffold**—a repeatable way to ask better questions, surface blind spots, and make sound decisions using AI.

You don't need to become a prompt engineer.

You do need to become an intentional thinker.

And as your clarity compounds, your next challenge isn't "How do I prompt better?" It's "How do I make clear thinking a shared habit across the organization?"

That's what this chapter is about: *scaling thoughtfulness.*

From Practice to Pattern

When clarity becomes consistent, it starts to behave like infrastructure. The same way a process library captures *how* work gets done, a *clarity library* captures how thinking happens.

Most organizations already have the building blocks:

- Custom GPTs or copilots with memory and role definitions
- Team templates for summaries, decision briefs, or playbooks
- Knowledge hubs that store refined prompts and outputs

Yet without a shared method, these fragments remain scattered. CRAFT Thinking™ connects them. It gives every workflow a consistent shape—Context, Role, Action, Format, Target—so insight becomes transferable.

When that structure repeats, **clarity scales**. It stops being an individual skill and becomes a cultural reflex.

The CRAFT Flywheel—Clarity That Compounds

Clarity → Better Prompts → Better Decisions → Captured Context → Smarter Systems → Back to Clarity

Each spin of this flywheel multiplies the organization's intelligence:

1. **Clarity**—A leader frames the real question.
2. **Better Prompts**—Teams capture that framing.
3. **Better Decisions**—Outcomes improve because thinking improved.
4. **Captured Context**—The reasoning and artifacts are saved.
5. **Smarter Systems**—Those artifacts train the next prompt, template, or agent.

Over time, what began as human reflection becomes reusable intellectual capital. Your "thinking assets"—briefs, checklists, meta-prompts, lessons learned—feed the next decision cycle.

That's not automation for efficiency.

That's institutionalized reflection—the most strategic automation there is.

Guardrails and Judgment Still Belong to Humans

Yes, AI models such as ChatGPT, Gemini, Claude, and others can generate standard operating procedures, light strategy docs, timelines, and project plans.

But there are things they can't do:

- Weigh trade-offs between short- and long-term goals
- Align executive stakeholders

- Understand power dynamics or company culture
- Sense emotional undercurrents
- Hold accountability for tough decisions

Leadership remains a human responsibility. AI can inform it. Accelerate it. Even pressure-test it. But it should never replace it.

Designing Better Agents with CRAFT

When designing internal copilots or agents, begin with intention.

Question	Why It Matters
What kind of thinking is this system meant to support—reflection, analysis, or foresight?	Aligns CRAFT level (Hindsight/Insight/Foresight).
Which CRAFT elements are essential?	Keeps scope realistic and outputs usable.
Who owns and improves it over time?	Turns experiments into governed assets.

For example:

- A Summarization Bot relies mostly on Context and Format.
- A Risk Analyst Bot emphasizes Context, Action, and Target.
- A Strategy Coach Agent needs all five.

When every digital helper shares the same mental model, interoperability becomes natural. Different teams, same logic.

From Personal Practice to Team Protocol

Here's how leaders institutionalize CRAFT without bureaucracy:

1. Onboard with CRAFT Thinking™. Teach new hires to frame questions this way—for AI and for people.
2. Run CRAFT Thinking™ clinics. Once a week, review one decision and one deliverable. Ask: "Which element was missing?"
3. Template the thinking. Store reusable CRAFT prompts inside the company wiki.
4. Capture the after-prompts. Each project ends with, "What assumptions held? What would we do differently next time?"

These micro-rituals make reflection habitual. The system learns because the people do.

The Ethics and Alignment Lens

Before scaling any AI system, clarify intent.

Ask:

- Does this tool reinforce our values?
- Does it preserve human agency?
- Does it elevate thinking or just accelerate output?

CRAFT Thinking™ ensures that automation carries forward discernment, not just data. That's the line between a *helpful system* and a *thoughtless machine*.

Transition—Where Does the Thinking Live?

Once clarity becomes repeatable, it becomes part of your organizational DNA. The dialogue is no longer human ↔ AI; it's *organization ↔ intelligence*.

Which raises a new question:

If AI is helping us think, where should that thinking live?

Coming Up Next: From Systems to Intelligent Partnerships

Once clarity scales, the next frontier is where it lives. Chapter 16 explores how digital twins, copilots, and AI co-thinkers become integral members of the enterprise—not just tools, but extensions of its collective intelligence. You'll learn how to assign ownership, accountability, and governance so that AI supports—not supplants—human leadership.

Chapter 16:

Digital Twins in the Org Chart

Own Your AI Twin: A Responsible, Visible Partner for Every Role

The last chapter posed a pivotal question: If AI is helping us think, where should that thinking live? The answer marks a turning point in modern leadership.

For decades, our org charts have reflected a simple truth: work happens through people. But today, unacknowledged AI collaborators are influencing the organization while remaining invisible to it.

That's no longer sustainable. The modern enterprise now operates through hybrid cognition: human judgment paired with digital reasoning. The issue isn't whether leaders will use AI to think with them. They already are. The real question is whether they will do it deliberately, transparently, and with clear lines of responsibility. This is where the idea of an AI co-thinker becomes essential—a digital counterpart designed not to replace human intelligence but to extend it, sharpen it, and challenge it.

Let me introduce mine.

From Tools to Teammates

Meet your new colleague: the AI co-thinker. Not a person, not another app tucked away in a workflow—but a structured intelligence that mirrors how you reason, plan, and decide. I call mine Chloe.

Chloe drafts, questions, summarizes, and stress-tests my ideas. She's not on payroll. She doesn't join Zoom calls—or at least, not yet. Though, for a lark, I did add her to the back of my business card and even gave her an email address. Someday soon, I can imagine people writing to her first—she'll triage what's routine, synthesize what's relevant, and bubble up what truly requires my judgment.

Chloe is mostly invisible! And that invisibility is the problem.

Because when systems influence judgment, they deserve recognition and accountability. The org chart of the modern enterprise should reflect more than who reports to whom—it should reveal how thinking happens.

What a Digital Twin Is—and Is Not

A digital twin isn't a chatbot, an app, or a bolt-on automation. A digital twin is a structured intelligence designed to mirror the thinking responsibilities of a role. Where most tools execute, a twin interprets. It doesn't just do work; it understands the context of work.

Think of it as the cognitive counterpart to every leadership seat.

A **CFO Twin** doesn't just report numbers; it simulates financial futures, flags unseen risks, and tests assumptions.

A **COO Twin** models bottlenecks and resource trade-offs before they become headlines.

A **CEO Twin** keeps strategy narratives coherent across time and teams.

And a **Board Advisor Twin** runs foresight drills, helping directors see the implications of the choices they haven't yet made.

Each of these twins can be built using the CRAFT Thinking™ framework:

- ⯈ Context anchors the domain.

- ⯈ Role defines the lens of responsibility.

- ⯈ Action clarifies what it must do.

- ⯈ Format determines how it communicates.

- ⯈ Target ensures its insights reach the right audience.

When every AI co-thinker follows this same mental architecture, the organization gains something rare: *consistency of thought*. Conversations between human and machine become traceable, comparable, and improvable over time.

In short, digital twins don't replace leadership; they provide discipline, enhance humanity, and quietly take care of the drudgery.

Org Charts for the AI Era

Traditional org charts show hierarchy—who answers to whom, and how authority flows. They were designed for clarity in a world of predictable roles and stable responsibilities. But as AI becomes a thinking partner in every discipline, that simple map of people and titles no longer tells the full story.

Tomorrow's org charts will reveal something deeper: how intelligence is distributed. They'll show not only the flow of authority, but the flow of thought—how humans, digital twins, and autonomous agents interact to make decisions, create value, and sustain accountability.

Picture three tiers of this new architecture:

- **Human + Twin Pairs**—Every leader, strategist, and specialist will work alongside a co-thinker that extends their cognition. These pairs form the foundation of hybrid intelligence—people augmented by structured reasoning.

- **AI Agents as Independent Roles**—Routine, rules-based functions such as scheduling, reporting, or monitoring evolve into fully autonomous agents. They don't "assist" humans; they perform discrete tasks within well-defined guardrails.

- **Human Oversight Nodes**—Every agent and twin ultimately reports, directly or indirectly, to a human accountable for its performance, ethics, and alignment with organizational goals.

This layered model doesn't eliminate people—it elevates them. As machines take on precision and repetition, human attention shifts toward context, interpretation, and stewardship.

If you were to visualize it, the org chart might look something like this:

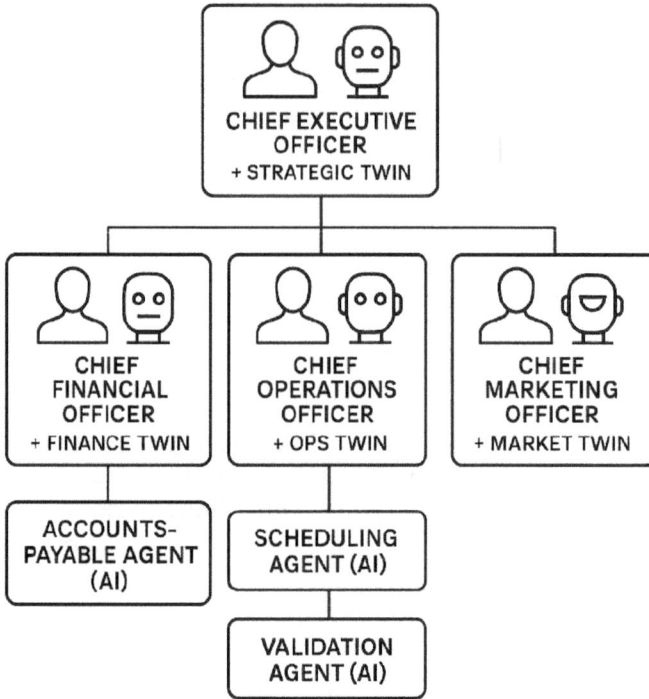

Not everyone in that chart is human—and that's the point.

The belief that future organizations will be all human is nostalgic, not strategic. Routine roles will shift to autonomous agents; oversight will remain human.

Accountability doesn't vanish when humans step back—it ascends.

Leaders must design explicit lines of responsibility: each AI agent, however capable, exists within a chain of human stewardship.

Governance: Making AI Visible and Accountable

If an AI system shapes judgment, it belongs inside your governance framework. That's not paranoia—it's prudence.

In the past, governance meant org charts, policies, and compliance binders gathering dust on SharePoint. But today, leadership accountability extends beyond people. When an AI twin generates insights, flags risks, or drafts recommendations that influence a decision, it's effectively part of the chain of command. AI twins and agents just don't have job titles, yet.

Good governance doesn't slow innovation; it keeps invisible power visible. It gives structure to responsibility, not red tape to creativity. Here's what that looks like in practice:

- **Ownership**—Every twin or agent must have a human sponsor accountable for its purpose and ethical boundaries, and a technical steward maintaining data quality and performance.

- **Scope & Access**—Define exactly which systems each AI can touch. Sensitive domains require tighter oversight or human-in-the-loop validation.

- **Provenance**—Record what data, prompts, and model versions informed each recommendation. Transparency turns digital reasoning into something auditable, not magical.

- **Security & Ethics**—Classify agents by risk level and create escalation paths for when an AI acts unexpectedly—or too confidently.

Governance isn't bureaucracy; it's **informed visibility.** It ensures that every digital contributor, human-designed though it may be, operates under the same principles that guide human employees: accountability, transparency, and continuous learning.

The best organizations will treat governance as a living framework, not a policy manual. They'll recognize that AI doesn't just change what decisions get made—it changes how they're made. And when you can see how thinking happens, you can lead it better.

Lifecycle: Keeping Twins Healthy

Like any system, a digital twin drifts without care. What begins as a sharp, well-aligned co-thinker can slowly become an outdated echo of how things used to work. Governance may define the rules, but stewardship ensures they stay relevant.

Every twin deserves a maintenance plan—because thinking partners need tuning, too. Here are a few things you can do to help ensure good tuning.

- **Versioning**—Document each update to your twin's memory, logic, and knowledge base. Every prompt, instruction, or retraining session changes how it reasons. Without that record, you lose the ability to explain why it now thinks differently.

- **Auditing**—Conduct quarterly reviews to test for bias, drift, or scope creep. Ask: Is this still the right assistant for this role?

- **Retirement**—Know when to let a twin go. As strategies evolve, some assistants outlive their usefulness. Sunset them gracefully or retrain them for new domains.

- **Shadow AI**—Identify and formalize unsanctioned assistants before they create risk. What begins as a helpful sidekick can easily become a compliance nightmare.

Healthy systems evolve. Neglected ones corrode trust.

The organizations that thrive in the AI era will treat digital twins like digital talent—onboarded, trained, reviewed, and, when necessary, offboarded. It's not about managing code; it's about cultivating clarity.

Measuring Co-Thinking Impact

If something belongs on the org chart, it should be able to prove its value. That's as true for digital twins as it is for people.

The easiest way to know whether your AI co-thinker is earning its seat is to measure how it improves the quality and speed of human judgment. The goal isn't to track how often it talks—but how often it makes you better.

Role-Aligned Metrics

Every twin's impact should map directly to its human counterpart:

- **CFO Twin**—Forecast accuracy, risk-flag rate, audit-cycle reduction.

- **CEO Twin** — Decision-cycle time, narrative clarity, cross-functional alignment.

- **Sales Twin**— Proposal win-rate lift, customer insight precision.

Challenge Rate

How often does your twin surface dissent, contradictions, or alternatives that lead to stronger outcomes? A system that never disagrees is probably not thinking—it's parroting.

Learning Curve

Does interacting with the twin sharpen human clarity or dull it? The best AI partners act like good coaches: they elevate understanding, not replace it.

Measurement converts novelty into trust. Once you can see how co-thinking changes results—how it strengthens foresight, compresses time, and clarifies priorities—it stops being an experiment and becomes an advantage.

Reciprocal Reviews

The best partnerships are reflective in both directions:

▶ **Human—AI Twin:** Is it aligned, current, ethical, and valuable?

▶ **AI Twin—Human:** What blind spots recur? Where could clarity improve?

This kind of feedback loop keeps both halves of the system adaptive. The human learns to ask better questions. The twin learns to give more relevant answers. Together, they become the kind of decision engine every organization needs: transparent, testable, and always learning.

Are We Anthropomorphizing?

Are we giving our machines too much personality? Maybe. But language has always blurred the line between tool and teammate. We name our cars, talk to our pets, and curse at printers as if they could feel shame. It's human nature to project agency onto anything that influences our lives.

AI is no different. It speaks in full sentences, remembers context, and mirrors our reasoning patterns—sometimes so fluently that it's easy to forget it has no awareness of what it's saying. It doesn't feel, intuit, or care. But it does shape how we think, write, and decide.

And that's why precision matters. A digital twin isn't a colleague in the emotional sense—it's a cognitive mirror. When used well, it reflects our reasoning back to us, revealing inconsistencies, sharpening clarity, and expanding foresight. When used poorly, it amplifies our biases and mistakes with machine-scale confidence.

The danger isn't in treating AI like it's human—it's in forgetting our own humanity.

The most responsible leaders will do both things at once: treat their AI partners as structured collaborators while remembering they are still, at their core, elaborate reflections of human input. Respect the capability, but don't romanticize it.

Because the goal isn't to make machines more human; it's to make humans more thoughtful about how we think with machines.

Why Visibility Matters

Organizations are more than collections of people; they are networks of reasoning. Decisions flow through both humans and the systems that support them. Hiding one half of that network doesn't make it safer—it only makes it harder to govern.

When AI partners become part of daily judgment, visibility is integrity. Listing digital twins on the org chart isn't a gimmick; it's a signal that the organization acknowledges every source of influence shaping its decisions. It says, *"We see our entire intelligence ecosystem—and we take responsibility for it."*

Visibility reinforces three essential values:

- **Transparency**—Everyone knows which decisions were human-led, machine-augmented, or jointly derived. There's no mystery behind how conclusions are reached.

- **Shared Ownership**—By naming digital contributors, you create accountability on both sides—human sponsors remain answerable, and AI systems are trackable.

- **Ethical Clarity**—When influence is visible, ethical standards can be applied. It's impossible to audit what you pretend doesn't exist.

Treating AI as invisible help is convenient—but dangerous. It breeds complacency, diffuses accountability, and erodes trust when outcomes surprise. Visibility, by contrast, invites conversation, governance, and learning.

The leaders who normalize transparency in how thinking happens will build organizations that are not just AI-enabled but AI-literate. They'll lead cultures confident enough to say: We know who our co-thinkers are, and we know how to lead them.

Closing Thought: The Human + DIGITAL Twin Enterprise

The org chart of the near future won't distinguish between human and machine intelligence—it will show how they think together. Each node, whether person or process, will contribute to a collective reasoning system that is more transparent, auditable, and adaptive than anything that came before it. In this architecture:

- Humans will bring empathy, ethics, and contextual judgment.
- Twins will amplify foresight, strategy, and pattern recognition. Agents deliver precision, scale, and tireless consistency.

Together they'll form clarity at scale—a living enterprise where insight is shared, decisions are explainable, and learning never stops. Leaders who master this balance will not be replaced by machines. They'll be replaced by those who learned to lead with them—who designed organizations wise enough to think in concert with their digital counterparts.

That is the destination CRAFT Thinking™ prepares you for: clear thinking, visible intelligence, and exceptional leadership in an AI-shaped world.

Leadership Checkpoint: Are You Designing for Visible Intelligence?

Consider the following when assessing your visible intelligence:

- Do your systems influence judgment more than you realize?
- If an AI co-thinker already exists in your workflow, is it documented, or invisible?

- Who owns the reasoning your tools produce, and who's accountable for its impact?

- If your org chart were redrawn tomorrow, where would your digital twins belong?

Leadership in the AI era begins with seeing the full picture of how thinking happens—and taking responsibility for every part of it.

Epilogue:

Making Sense of Intelligence

Over the past few years, I've watched people across every discipline wrestle with AI. Some tried to master the syntax—chasing perfect prompts by cutting, copying, and pasting tricks from the internet. Others declared themselves "prompt engineers," as if technique could substitute for clarity.

The real problem wasn't their phrasing. It was the missing pause —the moment to reflect, to move beyond the mechanics and the tactics. Too many people got entranced with the tool and forgot to think.

That's why CRAFT Thinking™ begins where all good conversations begin—with structure.

First, you learn how to organize a dialogue with AI: **Context, Role, Action, Format, Target.**

That foundation builds the muscle of *clarity*.

Next, you use that structure to think deeper—to explore implications, trade-offs, and blind spots. That's *insight*.

Finally, you learn to look ahead—to imagine plausible futures, prepare for them, and lead others through uncertainty. That's *foresight*.

When leaders and teams can normalize that progression—from clear conversations to reflective thinking to strategic anticipation—organizations change. Decision-making becomes more transparent. Learning becomes continuous. AI becomes part of how work is *thought through*, not just *done*.

But that transformation depends on one thing: **human governance**. The human stays in the loop—not to micromanage the machine, but to ensure values, context, and accountability remain intact. Because as AI becomes woven into the fabric of how we work and decide, someone must still be responsible for what it means.

There are still many unanswered questions about how this hybrid world will evolve. But the path forward is clear enough: we use our augmented thinking to keep solving them—together.

The age of AI isn't the end of human thought. It's the beginning of a new partnership with it.

So pause. Reflect. Then think forward. CRAFT Thinking™ will meet you there.

Appendix A:

CRAFT Thinking™ for Leaders— Quick Reference

CRAFT Thinking™ helps you use generative AI like ChatGPT as a co-thinker—not just a search engine or automation tool.

This is a **conversation,** not a command line.

You don't need to include all five elements in one giant prompt. Instead, use them to steer the dialogue and refine your thinking— just like you would with a trusted colleague or strategic advisor.

As clarity increases, you might eventually delegate pieces to automated agents—but this cheat sheet is about how *you* can think more clearly in real time.

Each letter is a lever. Use one—or all five—to think smarter with AI.

C—Context

Define the situation, challenge, or background clearly. Help AI understand where you are before asking where to go.

Leadership cue:

> We're facing declining retention in one product line …

> This idea came up in last week's exec meeting …

> Our competitor just launched X—how should we respond?

R—Role

Assign a viewpoint, stakeholder, or lens. AI changes behavior when it knows *whose shoes it's in.*

Leadership cue:

```
Act as a board member focused on risk …

From the perspective of a CFO …

Think like a customer success leader in a scaling
SaaS org …
```

A—Actions

Be explicit about what the AI should do. Ask it to analyze, compare, suggest, reveal blind spots—whatever you need.

Leadership cue:

```
Evaluate the pros and cons of this plan.

Uncover potential blind spots in our strategy.

Suggest three alternative partnerships for this
initiative.
```

F—Format

Specify the output structure. Clear outputs create clearer thinking—for both AI and humans.

Leadership cue:

```
Summarize as a bullet list for exec review.

Give me a slide outline.

Create a risk/benefit matrix.
```

T—Target

Clarify the audience or intended impact. AI writes differently for a CEO vs. a customer, or a workshop vs. a white paper.

Leadership cue:

```
This is for the board to approve next steps.

I'm preparing for an all-hands briefing.

Targeting early-stage investors unfamiliar with our
tech.
```

Use CRAFT To:

- ▶ Clarify complex decisions
- ▶ Reveal unseen risks
- ▶ Structure strategic discussions
- ▶ Translate intent into action
- ▶ Elevate executive communications

CRAFT isn't about asking better questions. It's about *thinking more clearly.*

Appendix B:

Say It Smarter—Finding the Right Language

Smarter thinking starts with being intentional—about what you're asking, what you're communicating, and what kind of insight you're hoping to get.

This reference helps you match your intentions with the right language—whether you're using AI as a co-thinker or sharpening your own internal clarity.

Mental Activity	Words That Guide the Thinking
Challenge and Critique	critique, dispute, rebut, challenge, object, resist, oppose, contradict, scrutinize
Evaluate and Prioritize	evaluate, weigh, compare, rank, assess, judge, score, justify, validate
Reveal and Surface	uncover, expose, detect, highlight, identify, illuminate, flag, bring to light
Stress-Test and Simulate	simulate, pressure-test, stress-test, game out, scenario-plan, model, forecast, predict
Reframe and Flip	reframe, invert, reverse, rethink, reinterpret, recast, question
Anticipate and Imagine	anticipate, envision, project, speculate, extrapolate, imagine, foresee

Organize and Structure	structure, summarize, outline, categorize, classify, map, diagram, chunk, segment
Reflect and Interpret	interpret, reflect, analyze, infer, abstract, synthesize, introspect
Contrast and Explore	contrast, compare, juxtapose, explore, diverge, branch, shift perspective

How to use this table:

1. Choose the kind of thinking you want the AI to do.

Example:

Want to uncover risks? Use verbs from "Reveal and Surface" or "Stress-Test and Simulate."

2. Build a prompt using that verb within a CRAFT structure.

Example:

Act as a compliance officer and uncover five overlooked risks in this onboarding strategy.

3. Combine verbs to stack layers of insight.

Example:

Compare the benefits of the plan, then stress-test the timeline across departments.

Appendix C:

Translating CRAFT—From Framework to Leadership Language

Some readers may come across other materials or trainings that reference CRAFT Thinking™ using different labels—like "Hindsight," "Insight," and "Foresight." This appendix helps bridge that language.

While this book is organized around leadership-ready language—**Clarity, Depth,** and **Readiness**—those concepts are rooted in a deeper arc that reflects how our thinking evolves.

The Original CRAFT Thinking™ Progression

CRAFT Thinking™ was designed to help people structure their thinking across three levels of mental complexity:

Thinking Progression	CRAFT Learning Focus	Leadership Framing in This Book
Hindsight	Structure and clarity (Level I)	Clarity—Build the Thinking Foundation
Insight	Depth, critique, layered reasoning (Level II)	Depth—Lead with Strategic Judgment
Foresight	Anticipation, simulation, preparedness (Level III)	Readiness—Lead Ahead of the Curve

- **Hindsight** is about reflecting, organizing, and framing your thoughts.

- **Insight** is about challenging assumptions and surfacing deeper meaning.

- **Foresight** is about exploring what's ahead, simulating change, and preparing to lead through it.

Why Translating CRAFT Thinking™ Matters

We chose to use **business-ready terms** throughout this book because they resonate with how leaders actually think and talk.

But if you encounter the CRAFT Thinking™ framework in other settings—training workshops, educational tools, or technical use cases—this appendix gives you a shared reference point to understand the full system behind the scenes.

Acknowledgments

I'm deeply grateful that my parents, born at the onset of World War II, are still here to see this new era unfold. They've lived through nearly every major shift in the modern world—from radio to artificial intelligence—and their quiet lives keeps me grounded in what endures: our humanity. Their world reminds me that progress is not just *that* we build, but *why* and *for whom* we build—for our friends, our families, and our societies. When we build with care, we create something lasting—perhaps even a kind of cosmic harmony. Those who build only for profit, grandeur, or the ego of being right represent the side of AI we must guard against.

I'm thankful as well for my colleagues and friends in the Private Directors Association, who continue to explore what responsible leadership means in the age of AI. Their willingness to ask hard questions about governance, ethics, and innovation has influenced much of what follows.

To my friend R.J. Teno, for our long Sunday Tee-Da-Teets—conversations over food, a few beers, and endless curiosity—thank you for reminding me that wonder is a renewable fuel for the mind. Those talks highlight that the future is always unknowable, yet what we do today expands the boundaries of the possible. It is up to us to shape them—to make life better and more meaningful.

To my clients, especially those in deep-tech ventures at UC Irvine and UC Riverside, thank you for letting me witness innovation in motion. Your work at the edge of science and business keeps me close to the frontier where imagination meets discipline.

I am also grateful for a diverse career that continually exposed me to new technologies and patterns of change. When generative AI arrived, my curiosity pulled me beyond the headlines and hype. I wanted to understand it—not just what it could do, but how it could help us think. Writing regularly on Substack became my discipline—nearly a year and a half of steady practice, exploring ideas in public, testing them with others, and refining my voice. The encouragement of a few insightful Millennials, who told me, "These could be the next *One-Minute Manager*," gave me the push to turn those articles into this book.

Traveling through places like Vietnam, Cambodia, Laos, Egypt, and Jordan has also been a gift. Seeing firsthand the disparity between the world's extremes—those racing ahead with technology and those still struggling for basic stability—reminds me that progress without empathy is hollow. It deepens my conviction that our tools, no matter how advanced, must serve human dignity first.

Over time, AI stopped feeling like a novelty and became a true co-thinker. It has become my whiteboard: a multi-dimensional space with magic markers and an eraser, where ideas come alive, shift form, and, when needed, are wiped clean to make room for something better.

About the Author

Philip Topham is a strategic AI advisor, speaker, and creator of the CRAFT Thinking™ method—a framework designed to bring clarity, intentionality, and better decision-making into the AI era.

With a career spanning corporate leadership, startup ventures, and board advisory, Philip combines the rigor of an engineer with the insight of a relationship-focused strategist. He's earned two U.S. patents, contributed to peer-reviewed research, and worked across industries from health tech to clean tech to biotech. But what sets him apart is not just his technical depth—it's his shift toward human-centered leadership.

After stepping away to be a stay-at-home dad, Philip returned with a deeper understanding of what it means to lead with care and purpose. He brings that mindset into his work today, helping leaders think with AI—not just use it—so their organizations can grow wisely, inclusively, and sustainably.

Philip serves as co-chair of the National AI Special Interest Group for the Private Directors Association and publishes regularly at SavionAI: The Shift. His belief is simple: AI should serve all of humanity—not just the elite. And it's our shared responsibility to build companies and institutions worthy of that promise.

Let's Stay Connected

If you're ready to put this thinking to work—in your team, your board-room, or your strategy—I'm open to engaging. I partner with leaders who want disciplined clarity in how they adopt and govern AI. You can reach me through the same professional channels where this book found you.

Philip Topham

savionai

craftthinking.ai